Self-Renewal

THE INDIVIDUAL AND THE INNOVATIVE SOCIETY

Revised Edition

Books by John W. Gardner

SELF-RENEWAL: *The Individual and the Innovative Society*
EXCELLENCE: *Can We Be Equal and Excellent Too?*
NO EASY VICTORIES
THE RECOVERY OF CONFIDENCE
IN COMMON CAUSE
MORALE
(With Francesca G. Reese) QUOTATIONS OF
WIT AND WISDOM

Self-Renewal

THE INDIVIDUAL
AND THE INNOVATIVE SOCIETY

Revised Edition

By John W. Gardner

W · W · NORTON & COMPANY

NEW YORK   LONDON

Library of Congress Cataloging-in-Publication Data
Gardner, John W., 1912–
Self-renewal.
Includes bibliographical references and index.
1. Progress. 2. Self-help. I. Title.
HM101.G27   1981   303.4   81-4680

ISBN 0-393-31295-X

W. W. Norton & Company, Inc.
500 Fifth Avenue, New York, N.Y. 10110
www.wwnorton.com

W. W. Norton & Company Ltd.
Castle House, 75/76 Wells Street, London W1T 3QT

5 7 9 0 8 6 4

FOR AIDA

CONTENTS

FOREWORD

Heraclitus observed that "No one steps twice into the same river"; and twenty-five centuries later thinkers are still rediscovering the inescapable reality of change. Life and the world keep flowing and evolving.

Surely by now we grasp that truth. But we are of two minds as to whether we like it. There's something in us that fiercely resists change. And there's something else in us that welcomes it, finds it bracing, even seeks it out. It's the latter trait that keeps the species going.

Failure to face the realities of change brings heavy penalties. Individuals become imprisoned in their own rigidities. Great institutions deteriorate. Civilizations fall. Yet decay is not inevitable. There is also renewal.

I shall discuss, among other things, the decay and renewal of organizations and societies; but this is above all a book about the individual. Individuals create societies and make them vital; and individuals bring them to moldering ruin. So this is a book about you.

It's a book about the things that hem you in and the things

that liberate you. It's about coping with change. It's about the loss and renewal of vitality.

The factors that produce deterioration are powerful and universally applicable. They can be countered but they cannot be wished out of existence. Nor can they be held at bay by wealth, power or status—or any of the guarantees of worldly security. Indeed, one is tempted to say that deterioration sets in most quickly where worldly security seems most assured.

For men and women who have accepted the reality of change, the need for endless learning and trying is a way of living, a way of thinking, a way of being awake and ready. Life isn't a train ride where you choose your destination, pay your fare and settle back for a nap. It's a cycle ride over uncertain terrain, with you in the driver's seat, constantly correcting your balance and determining the direction of progress. It's difficult, sometimes profoundly painful. But it's better than napping through life.

When I wrote the first edition of *Self-Renewal* I was concerned with the universal sources of personal and social vitality and decay. The principles involved have not changed in any particular since that edition appeared. What I wrote then stands substantially as I wrote it. But having lived with the subject for some years, there are topics in the book that I wish to underscore and comment on; and I shall do so in this foreword.

Though the book suggests that renewal depends on many factors, I would point to one as uniquely important—motivation. If people are apathetic, defeated in spirit, or unable to imagine a future worth striving for, the game is lost. It is worth exploring at some length how we may spare ourselves such a collapse of spirit and will.

First, I would stress the importance of a toughminded optimism. Both the toughmindedness and the optimism are immensely important. High hopes that are dashed by the first failure are precisely what we don't need. We need to believe in ourselves but not to believe that life is easy. Nothing in the historical record tells us that triumph is assured. Life's problems resist solution, and we are fallible.

But to say there is no assurance of success is one thing: to give up in despair is something else. In *War and Peace*, Prince Andrei said of Austerlitz, "We lost because we told ourselves we lost." Militarily it wasn't that simple, but the point is clear.

The future is shaped by men and women with a steady, even zestful, confidence that on balance their efforts will not have been in vain. They take failure and defeat not as reason to doubt themselves but as reason to strengthen resolve. Some combination of hope, vitality and indomitability makes them willing to bet their lives on ventures of unknown outcome. If our forebears had all looked before they leaped, we would still be crouched in caves sketching animal pictures on the wall.

Second, I would emphasize staying power. Stamina is an attribute rarely celebrated by the poets, but it has had a good deal to do with the history of humankind. And with the life history of each person.

Nothing is ever finally safe. Life is tumultuous—an endless losing and regaining of balance, a continuous struggle, never an assured victory. We need a hardbitten morale that enables us to face these truths and still strive with every ounce of our energy to prevail.

But there is no possibility of sustaining ourselves in that effort if our values and beliefs are so weakened that nothing seems worth the struggle. First and last, humans live by ideas that validate their striving, ideas that say it's worth living and trying. What makes a collection of people a society is the cohesiveness that stems out of shared values, purposes and beliefs.

Every year millions of Americans come to Washington to visit our national shrines—the Lincoln Memorial, the Washington Monument, the Capitol. But the spirit of the nation does not reside in the physical structures. It is in the minds of the citizens who come to look at the structures. That is where a vital society begins; and, if it ends, that is where it will end. If they stop believing, if they lose faith, if they stop caring, the monuments will be meaningless piles of stone, and the venture that began with the Declaration of Independence, the venture familiarly known as America, will be as lifeless as the stone.

It could happen, but it need not. Just as shared beliefs and values are susceptible to decay, so are they capable of regeneration. Humans are not without talent in the creation and renewal of value systems. It may be their most distinctive activity. But in a world of swift change it calls for unrelenting effort.

In earlier times one generation might create value patterns that several following generations would live by unquestioningly. It was as though one generation built the houses, and succeeding generations lived in them, forgetting their own building skills in the process. Today we are more like people in a land of recurring earthquakes and tornadoes, where each generation must keep its building skills fresh and in fact rebuild almost continuously.

Most of what I have said so far bears on individual attitudes and values. Beyond that the book deals with the institutional arrangements and processes that affect renewal. I shall limit myself in this foreword to a few brief comments on the subject.

Our Founding Fathers handed us a system superbly designed for continuous renewal. A totalitarian regime may accomplish a spectacular short burst of social change. But there cannot be long-continued renewal without liberty, pluralism and regard for the worth of the individual.

Liberty requires the limiting and disciplining of power. Over the centuries, humans have tried diverse means of achieving that end, and two strategies have emerged as superior to all others. One is the creation of institutional arrangements and laws (the Constitution, for example) designed to place constraints on power.

The other strategy is to disperse power; since this has important implications for renewal, I shall dwell on it at greater length. In our own society, provision is made for the separation of powers, checks and balances, universal suffrage, a lively and independent private sector, markets, private property, and various forms of participation beyond voting. Dispersing power is an endless task: it never stays dispersed for long. In authoritarian systems, of course, it never gets dispersed at all.

No matter how many checks and balances we build into government, the abuse of power remains an ever-present possibility. So there must be bases of power and forceful voices outside of government; and the private sector can provide such bases. It can preserve an arena into which the long arm of political power can reach only so far. It is the seedbed and greenhouse of the pluralism we value so highly.

Pluralism is a social strategy that encourages the existence of many sources of initiative, many kinds of institutions, many conflicting beliefs, many competing economic units. In authoritarian political systems there is one dominant source of power and initiative, one ideology, one "correct" answer.

Within our pluralistic system, citizens can create new forms of association, unpopular ideas can be expressed, religious groups can pursue their deepest convictions, great institutions of learning can function independently, and all kinds of profit and nonprofit ventures can flourish or fail.

The most widely recognized participants in the private sector are those involved directly in the economic functions of the society—business people, farmers, union members. But there is today a new awareness of the nonprofit segment of the private sector. Like the profit segment, its institutions are extravagantly pluralistic—hospitals, museums, religious groups, civic organizations, great universities, citizen groups, scientific laboratories, social service agencies and so on.

In its size and diversity the nonprofit world is uniquely American; it stems from a deeply ingrained American habit of forming voluntary associations whenever a purpose might be achieved through joint action.

The sector is a significant source of renewal. An idea that is controversial, unpopular or strange has little chance in either the commercial or the political marketplace. But in the nonprofit sector it may very well find the few followers necessary to nurse it to maturity. The sector comfortably harbors innovators, maverick movements, groups which feel that they must fight for their place in the sun, and critics and dissenters of both liberal and conservative persuasion. And it is from just such individuals and groups that one may expect emergence of the ideas that will dominate our society and our world a century hence. Generally speaking, great social changes begin with few supporters.

Over the years, even a very successful society may have to seek new solutions. Just as a species has in the genes of its members a great storehouse of possibilities for future adaptation, a society must have within itself a range of alternatives for possible future use. New ideas and new ways of doing things test the validity of currently accepted doctrine and build an inventory of possible alternative solutions to be used if circumstances change. Therein lies the relevance of pluralism to the renewal of societies.

A tradition of vigorous criticism is essential to the renewal of a society. A nation is not helped much by citizens whose love for their country leads them to shield it from life-giving criticism. But neither is it helped much by critics without love, skilled in demolition but unskilled in the arts by which human institutions are nurtured and strengthened and made to flourish. Neither uncritical lovers nor unloving critics make for the renewal of societies.

In our tradition any group of citizens may identify a problem, offer a solution and attempt to persuade the rest of the nation of its rightness. The fruitfulness of the tradition may be seen in the historic contribution of citizen groups to Abolitionism, Populism, the vote for women, child labor laws, environmentalism and the civil rights movements. It is not too much to assert that almost every historic shift in policy in the past century has come out of voluntary associations.

Citizens may not always be wise. And they may not always be successful in persuading their fellow citizens. For every citizen movement that changes the course of history, there are many thousands that hardly create a ripple. The few movements that survive are those that speak to the authentic concerns of substantial numbers of people.

In this perspective, the people are a fertile seedbed. Ideas are the seedlings. Some never germinate. Some die early. A few prosper and grow strong. The whole process provides the society with a superb source of new growth. It offers ample opportunity for the testing of ideas—good ideas, ordinary ideas, dismal ideas. Only the ideas with a powerful popular impact will affect history. The great virtue of a free people is to be that fertile seedbed, not—as some have supposed—to be always right or enlightened but to be the soil from which enlightenment can spring.

But the capacity to germinate is in the individual seed. And the source of creativity for the society is in the person. Renewal springs from the freshness and vitality of individual men and women. That is the theme that runs through the book.

INTRODUCTION

As I was browsing in a university bookstore recently, I heard an apple-cheeked girl say to her companion, "The truth is that our society and everything in it is in a state of decay." I studied her carefully, and I must report that she did not seem even slightly decayed. But what of the society as a whole?

Decay is hardly the word for what is happening to us. We are witnessing changes so profound and far-reaching that the mind can hardly grasp all the implications. With respect to most of these events—space exploration is the spectacular example—we are not just passive observers but are helping to produce the changes. That is a story of dynamism, not deterioration.

Yet no one can fail to see in some segments of our society the dry rot produced by apathy, by rigidity and by moral emptiness. Only the blind and complacent could fail to recognize the great tasks of renewal facing us—in government, in education, in race relations, in urban redevelopment, in international affairs, and most of all in our own minds and hearts.

In my earlier book, *Excellence,* I stressed the importance of high standards.* But high standards are not enough. There are kinds of excellence—very important kinds—that are not necessarily associated with the capacity for renewal. A society that has reached heights of excellence may already be caught in the rigidities that will bring it down. An institution may hold itself to the highest standards and yet already be entombed in the complacency that will eventually spell its decline.

We are beginning to understand the processes of growth and decline in societies. We understand better than ever before how and why an aging society loses its adaptiveness and stifles creativity in its members. And we are beginning to comprehend the conditions under which a society may renew itself.

But social renewal depends ultimately on individuals; and the individual today has his problems. In a recent television drama a mad scientist, sitting before the control panel of his computer, declared, "The individual is obsolete. We can survive only if society runs like a finely tuned machine. That requires suppression of individuality."

Many people today fear that such echoes of Orwell and Huxley are an accurate omen of things to come. They doubt that individuality in the old sense can survive the complex and impersonal demands of modern mass society. The danger is real, and we must combat it with all the resources at our command. Fortunately, those resources are substantial. We now know a great deal about the hazards to the individual in modern society, and we know how to prevent some of them.

---

* Hereafter, superior numbers will refer to a section of notes beginning on page 129.

We need not be enslaved by the organizational arrangements we have designed to serve us.

If a society hopes to achieve renewal, it will have to be a hospitable environment for creative men and women. It will also have to produce men and women with the capacity for self-renewal. Thanks to recent research, we now know a good deal about the creative person and about the environment which fosters creativity. As for self-renewal, we know that men and women need not fall into a stupor of mind and spirit by the time they are middle-aged. They need not relinquish as early as they do the resilience of youth and the capacity to learn and grow. Self-renewal is possible.

But renewal—of societies or of individuals—depends in some measure on motivation, commitment, conviction, the values men live by, the things that give meaning to their lives. E. A. Sothern, the great nineteenth-century actor, was observing a small boy who wanted to go outdoors to join his older playmates but feared they would not accept him. When the children started to return to the house, Sothern said playfully, "Let's hide behind the curtain and they won't know where we are!" The boy looked at him disconsolately and said, "Suppose they don't care?"

It is a question that must be asked of every social enterprise. The renewal of societies and organizations can go forward only if someone cares. Apathy and lowered motivation are the most widely noted characteristics of a civilization in decline. Apathetic men and women accomplish nothing. Those who believe in nothing change nothing for the better. They renew nothing and heal no one, least of all themselves. Anyone who understands our situation at all knows that we are in little danger of failing through lack of material strength. If we falter, it will be a failure of heart and spirit.

Books that discuss creativity do not ordinarily discuss moral decay and renewal. Books on social organization do not usually examine the individual's capacity for lifelong learning. I have not brought these topics together with the essayist's inclination to ramble. I have brought them together because they are all parts of the same problem. Unless we attend to the requirements of renewal, aging institutions and organizations will eventually bring our civilization to moldering ruin. Unless we cope with the ways in which modern society oppresses the individual, we shall lose the creative spark that renews both societies and men. Unless we foster versatile, innovative and self-renewing men and women, all the ingenious social arrangements in the world will not help us.

Finally, we shall renew neither ourselves, nor our society, nor a troubled world unless we share a vision of something worth saving. Today the road ahead is clouded by the danger of nuclear war, and the enormity of the threat blocks our vision. We have the difficult task of facing the threat and at the same time looking beyond it. If we fail to look beyond it, the long-term future will lose all reality for us, and we shall forget what kind of world we might have wished to build had we been granted peace.

Self-Renewal

THE INDIVIDUAL AND THE INNOVATIVE SOCIETY

Revised Edition

CHAPTER 1

GROWTH, DECAY AND

RENEWAL

THE EVER-RENEWING SYSTEM

Every few years the archaeologists unearth another ancient civilization that flourished for a time and then died. The modern mind, acutely conscious of the sweep of history and chronically apprehensive, is quick to ask, "Is it our turn now?"

Rather than debate that overworked topic, I am going to ask another kind of question: "Suppose one tried to imagine a society that would be relatively immune to decay—an ever-renewing society. What would it be like? What would be the ingredients that provide the immunity?"

We now know enough about the nature of human organization to specify the ingredients of such a society—not one that will last forever, but one that will extend its vitality far beyond the usual span.

If longevity were the only virtue of such a society, the whole venture might prove to be numbingly dull. But a society that has learned the secret of renewal will be a more interesting and more vibrant society, not in some distant future but at once. And since continuous renewal depends on conditions that encourage fulfillment of the individual, it will be a society fit for free men and women.

Though the only society that can renew itself over a long period of time is a free society, this offers no grounds for complacency. We are not living up to our ideals as a free society, and we are very far from meeting the requirements of an ever-renewing society. But both are within reach.

Neither the popular nor the scholarly theories that have sought to explain the rise and fall of civilizations have stood up under critical scrutiny.[1] But the Spenglers and Toynbees of the future need not despair. We are just now discovering facts about institutional growth and decay that will make better theories possible.

It is not a subject in which simple generalizations will ever be possible. Patterns of growth and decay vary from one society to another. Various kinds of renewal disrupt the simple "rise and fall" trajectory. A decaying society may have exceedingly vital elements within it, and the vital society is never free from decay. In short, we are talking about processes of great complexity—but not so complex as to defy understanding.

It is necessary to discuss not only the vitality of societies but the vitality of institutions and individuals. They are the same subject. A society decays when its institutions and individuals lose their vitality.

Recently a government official, describing an old-line government agency, said, "It doesn't get much public attention, and it has gone quietly to sleep. When there is a change of administration, it stirs fitfully—but it doesn't wake up." Every businessman knows of some firms that are "on their toes" and others that are "in a rut." Every university president recognizes that some academic departments are enjoying exceptional vitality while others have gone to seed.

What are the factors that account for such differences? It is a question that has never been examined systematically. Closer study will reveal that in all the examples given the same processes are at work. They are the processes involved in the rise and fall of human institutions. Rome falling to the barbarians, an old family firm going into bankruptcy, and a government agency quietly strangling in its own red tape have more in common than one might suppose.

When organizations and societies are young, they are flexible, fluid, not yet paralyzed by rigid specialization and willing to try anything once. As the organization or society ages, vitality diminishes, flexibility gives way to rigidity, creativity fades and there is a loss of capacity to meet challenges from unexpected directions. Call to mind the adaptability of youth, and the way in which that adaptability diminishes with the years. Call to mind the vigor and recklessness of some new organizations and societies—our own frontier settlements, for example—and reflect on how frequently these qualities are buried under the weight of tradition and history.

Similarly infants are models of openness to new experience —receptive, curious, eager, unafraid, willing to try anything and above all not inhibited by settled habits and attitudes. As the years pass they lose these priceless qualities. Inevitably they acquire fixed ways of doing things. If they did not, they would remain infantile and wholly incapable of coping with their environment. But each acquired attitude or habit, useful though it may be, makes them less receptive to alternative ways of thinking and acting. They become more competent to function in their own environment, less adaptive to changes.

All of this seems to suggest that the critical question is how to stay young. But youth implies immaturity. And though everyone wants to be young, no one wants to be immature. Unfortunately, as many a youth-seeker has learned, the two are intertwined.

Most of the processes that reduce the initial flexibility and adaptiveness of societies and individuals are, in fact, processes of maturing. As such they are not only inevitable but, in their early stages, desirable. The process of maturing may have made our frontier communities less vigorous and venturesome, but it also made them more livable, more orderly and in important respects stronger. Everyone who has ever shared in the founding of an organization looks back with nostalgia on the early days of confusion and high morale, but few would really enjoy a return to that primitive level of functioning. Babies are charming but no one would wish to keep them forever at that stage of growth.

In short, we would not want to stop the process of maturing even though it narrows potentialities and reduces adaptability.

The reader may ask, "Is there no possibility, then, that an individual (or an organization or society) might advance toward maturity without advancing toward rigidity and senility? Isn't it a question of knowing the difference between the two and stopping short of the latter?" Unfortunately, it isn't that simple. There may be a point at which raw young vitality and mature competence and wisdom reach a kind of ideal balance, but there is no possibility of freezing change at that point, as one might stop the motion in a home movie. There is nothing static in these processes.

Does this mean that there is no alternative to eventual stagnation? It does not. Every individual, organization or society must mature, but much depends on how this maturing takes place. A society whose maturing consists simply of acquiring more firmly established ways of doing things is headed for the graveyard—even if it learns to do these things with greater and greater skill. *In the ever-renewing society what matures is a system or framework within which continuous innovation, renewal and rebirth can occur.*

Our thinking about growth and decay is dominated by the image of a single life-span, animal or vegetable. Seedling, full flower and death. "The flower that once has blown forever dies." But for an ever-renewing society the appropriate image is a total garden, a balanced aquarium or other ecological system. Some things are being born, other things are flourishing, still other things are dying—but the system lives on.

Over the centuries the classic question of social reform has been, "How can we cure this or that specifiable ill?" Now we must ask another kind of question: "How can we design a system that will continuously reform (i.e., renew) itself, beginning with presently specifiable ills and moving on to ills that we cannot now foresee?"

Something Old, Something New

A modern view of the processes of growth, decay and renewal must give due emphasis to both continuity and change in human institutions.

It is not true, as some seem to believe, that awareness of change is a twentieth-century development. Nicholas Murray Butler used to insist that in the Garden of Eden, Adam paused at one point to say, "Eve, we are living in a period of transition." But no sensible person would assert that earlier centuries experienced change as the twentieth century has experienced it. A radical speeding up of the tempo of change is at the heart of the twentieth-century experience and has gained a powerful grip on the modern mind.

Many Americans have a sentimental and undiscriminating view of change. They think it is, without qualification, a good thing. But death is a form of change. So is deterioration. A society must court the kinds of change that will enrich and strengthen it, rather than the kinds that will fragment and destroy it. Who among us has not been startled in recent years by instances of runaway growth, of expansion so rapid that it outruns all control. Faced with such instances, even the most forward-looking person may be forgiven for thinking: "This is change gone wild. This is growth so destructive of other values as to be cancerous!"

Renewal is not just innovation and change. It is also the process of bringing the results of change into line with our purposes. When our forbears invented the motor car, they had to devise rules of the road. Both are phases of renewal. When urban expansion threatens chaos, we must revise our conceptions of city planning and metropolitan government.

Mesmerized as we are by the idea of change, we must guard against the notion that continuity is a negligible—if not reprehensible—factor in human history. It is a vitally important ingredient in the life of individuals, organizations and societies. Particularly important to a society's continuity are its long-term purposes and values. These purposes and values also evolve in the long run; but by being relatively durable, they enable a society to absorb change without losing its distinctive character and style. They do much to determine the direction of change. They insure that a society will not be buffeted in all directions by every wind that blows.

A sensible view of these matters sees an endless interweaving of continuity and change. The scientist engaged in momentous innovations in his laboratory may seem to be the personification of change, yet he functions effectively because of certain deeply established continuities in his life. As a scientist he is living out a tradition several centuries old in its modern incarnation, thousands of years old in its deeper roots. Every move he makes reflects attitudes, habits of mind and skills that were years in the making. He is part of an enduring tradition and a firmly established intellectual system; but it is *a system that provides for its own continuous renewal.*

This brings us to the modern emphasis on process, an emphasis suggested, in its broadest implications, by Arnold Toynbee when he said, "Civilization is a movement . . . and not a condition, a voyage and not a harbor."[2]

Emphasis on process—and the complex interweaving of continuity and change—plays havoc with old-fashioned conceptions of liberalism and conservatism. As Peter Drucker has pointed out, in a world buffeted by change, faced daily with new threats to its safety, the only way to conserve is by innovating.[3] The only stability possible is stability in motion.

CHAPTER 2

SELF-RENEWAL

Do-It-Yourself Jailbirds

"Keep on growing," the commencement speakers say. "Don't go to seed. Let this be a beginning, not an ending."

It is a good theme. Yet a high proportion of the young people who hear the speeches pay no heed, and by the time they are middle-aged they are absolutely mummified. Even some of the people who make the speeches are mummified. Why?

Unfortunately the commencement speakers never tell us why their advice to keep on learning is so hard to follow. The people interested in adult education have struggled heroically to increase the *opportunities* for self-development, and they have succeeded marvelously. Now they had better turn to the thing that is really blocking self-development—the individual's own intricately designed, self-constructed prison, or to put it another way, the individual's incapacity for self-renewal.

A prison is not quite the appropriate image because the

8

individual does not stop learning in all aspects of his life simultaneously. Many young people have stopped learning in the religious or spiritual dimensions of their lives long before they graduate from college. Some settle into rigid and unchanging political and economic views by the time they are twenty-five or thirty. By their mid-thirties most will have stopped acquiring new skills or new attitudes in any central aspect of their lives.

As we mature we progressively narrow the scope and variety of our lives. Of all the interests we might pursue, we settle on a few. Of all the people with whom we might associate, we select a small number. We become caught in a web of fixed relationships. We develop set ways of doing things.[1]

As the years go by we view our familiar surroundings with less and less freshness of perception. We no longer look with a wakeful, perceiving eye at the faces of people we see every day, nor at any other features of our everyday world.

That is why travel is a vivid experience for most of us. At home we have lost the capacity to see what is before us. Travel shakes us out of our apathy, and we regain an attentiveness that heightens every experience.[2] The exhilaration of travel has many sources, but surely one of them is that we recapture in some measure the unspoiled awareness of children.

It is not unusual to find that the major changes in life— marriage, a move to a new city, a change of jobs or a national emergency—break the patterns of our lives and reveal to us quite suddenly how much we had been imprisoned by the comfortable web we had woven around ourselves. Unlike the jailbird, we don't know that we've been imprisoned until after we've broken out.

It was a characteristic experience during the Second World War that men and women who had been forced to break the pattern of their lives often discovered within themselves resources and abilities they had not known to exist. How ironic that it should take war and disaster to bring about self-renewal on a large scale! It is an expensive way to accomplish it.

When we have learned to achieve such self-renewal without wars and other disasters, we shall have discovered one of the most important secrets a society can learn, a secret that will unlock new resources of vitality throughout the society.[3] And we shall have done something to avert the hardening of the arteries that attacks so many societies. People who have lost their adaptiveness naturally resist change. The most stubborn protectors of their own vested interest are those who have lost the capacity for self-renewal.[4]

SELF-DEVELOPMENT

No one knows why some individuals seem capable of self-renewal while others do not. But we have some important clues to what the self-renewing person is like, and what we might do to foster renewal.[5]

For self-renewing men and women the development of their own potentialities and the process of self-discovery never end. It is a sad but unarguable fact that most people go through their lives only partially aware of the full range of their abilities. As a boy in California I spent a good deal of time in the Mother Lode country, and like every boy of my age I listened raptly to the tales told by the old-time prospectors in that area, some of them veterans of the Klondike gold rush. Every one of them had at least one good campfire story of a lost gold mine. The details varied: the original discoverer had died in the mine, or had gone crazy, or had been killed in a shooting scrape, or had just walked off thinking the mine worthless. But the central theme was constant: riches left untapped. I have come to believe that those tales offer a paradigm of education as most of us experience it. The mine is worked for a little while and then abandoned.

The development of abilities is at least in part a dialogue between individuals and their environment. If they have the ability and the environment demands it, it will surely develop. The young person with excellent athletic skills is likely to discover that ability fairly early. Almost any child with the gift for charming grown-ups will have no trouble discovering that talent. But most abilities are not so readily evoked by the common circumstances of life. The "mute, inglorious Miltons" are more numerous than one might suppose, particularly in an age in which even an articulate Milton might go unnoticed, certainly unrewarded. Most of us have potentialities that have never been developed simply because the circumstances of our lives never called them forth.

Exploration of the full range of our own potentialities is not something that we can safely leave to the chances of life. It is something to be pursued systematically, or at least avidly, to the end of our days. We should look forward to an endless and unpredictable dialogue between our potentialities and the claims of life—not only the claims we encounter but the claims we invent. And by potentialities I mean not just skills, but the full range of our capacities for sensing, wondering, learning, understanding, loving and aspiring.

The ultimate goal of the educational system is to shift to

the individual the burden of pursuing his own education. This will not be a widely shared pursuit until we get over our odd conviction that education is what goes on in school buildings and nowhere else. Not only does education continue when schooling ends, but it is not confined to what may be studied in adult education courses. The world is an incomparable classroom, and life is a memorable teacher for those who aren't afraid of her.

The society can do much to encourage such self-development. The most important thing it can do is to remove the obstacles to individual fulfillment. This means doing away with the gross inequalities of opportunity imposed on some of our citizens by prejudice, poverty and other handicaps. And it means a continuous and effective operation of "talent salvage" to assist young people to achieve the promise that is in them. The benefits are not only to the individual but to the society. The renewing society must be continuously refreshed by a stream of new talent from all segments or strata of society. Nothing is more decisive for social renewal than the mobility of talent.

SELF-KNOWLEDGE

But the discovery of talent is only one side, perhaps the easier side, of self-development. The other side is self-knowledge. The maxim "Know thyself"—so ancient . . . so deceptively simple . . . so difficult to follow—has gained in richness of meaning as we learn more about human nature. Even today only the wisest of people have an inkling of all that is implied in that gnomic saying. Research in psychology and psychiatry has shown the extent to which mental health is bound up in a reasonably objective view of the self, in accessibility of the self to consciousness, and in acceptance of the self. Erikson has helped us to understand how crucial and how perilous is the young person's search for identity.[6]

We cannot explore here the full implications of these views. Nor can we even begin to examine the various psychological conditions that facilitate or obstruct self-renewal. It would be interesting to examine the manner in which life's blows and brutalities cause a tough scar tissue to form over naturally responsive spirits. It would be useful to examine the processes by which fears and anxieties cut us off from some of life's deepest experiences—a kind of imprisonment that is no less so for being "protective custody." But these topics would take us far afield.

Josh Billings said, "It is not only the most difficult thing to know oneself, but the most inconvenient one, too." Human beings have always employed an enormous variety of clever devices for running away from themselves, and the modern world is particularly rich in such stratagems. We can keep ourselves so busy, fill our lives with so many diversions, stuff our heads with so much knowledge, involve ourselves with so many people and cover so much ground that we never have time to probe the fearful and wonderful world within. More often than not we don't want to know ourselves, don't want to depend on ourselves, don't want to live with ourselves. By middle life most of us are accomplished fugitives from ourselves.

A long, long time ago George Herbert said:

> By all means use some times to be alone.
> Salute thyself: see what thy soul doth wear.[7]

That is good self-renewal doctrine. The individual who has become a stranger to himself has lost the capacity for genuine self-renewal. He can no longer return for sustenance to the springs of his own being.

Niebuhr has written:

> The conquest of self is in a sense the inevitable consequence of true self-knowledge. If the self-centered self is shattered by a genuine awareness of its situation, there is the power of a new life in the experience.[8]

COURAGE TO FAIL

One of the reasons mature people are apt to learn less than young people is that they are willing to risk less. Learning is a risky business, and they do not like failure. In infancy, when children are learning at a phenomenal rate—a rate they will never again achieve—they are also experiencing a great many failures. Watch them. See the innumerable times they try and fail. See how little the failures discourage them. With each year that passes they will be less blithe about failure. By adolescence the willingness of young people to risk failure has diminished greatly. And all too often parents push them further along that road by instilling fear, by punishing failure or by making success seem too precious. By middle age most of us carry in our heads a tremendous catalogue of things we have no intention of trying again because we tried them once and failed—or tried them once and did less well than our self-esteem demanded.

One of the virtues of formal schooling is that it requires the student to test himself in a great variety of activities that are not of his own choosing. But the adult can usually select the kinds of activity on which he allows himself to be tested, and he takes full advantage of that freedom of choice. He tends increasingly to confine himself to the things he does well and to avoid the things in which he has failed or has never tried.

We pay a heavy price for our fear of failure. It is a powerful obstacle to growth. It assures the progressive narrowing of the personality and prevents exploration and experimentation. There is no learning without some difficulty and fumbling. If you want to keep on learning, you must keep on risking failure—all your life. It's as simple as that. When Max Planck was awarded the Nobel Prize he said:

> Looking back . . . over the long and labyrinthine path which finally led to the discovery [of the quantum theory], I am vividly reminded of Goethe's saying that men will always be making mistakes as long as they are striving after something.[9]

Love

Another attribute of self-renewing people is that they have mutually fruitful relations with others. They are capable of accepting love and of giving it—both more difficult achievements than is commonly thought. They are capable of depending on others and of being depended upon. They can see life through another's eyes and feel it through another's heart.

And what has this to do with self-renewal? The man or woman who cannot achieve these relationships is imprisoned, cut off from a great part of the world of experience. The joy and suffering of those we love are part of our own experience. We feel their triumphs and defeats, their hopes and fears, their anger and pity, and our lives are richer for it.

But vicarious experience is a minor consequence of love.

Love and friendship dissolve the rigidities of the isolated self, force new perspectives, alter judgments and keep in working order the emotional substratum on which all profound comprehension of human affairs must rest.

MOTIVATION

The self-renewing person is highly motivated. The walls that hem us in as we grow older form channels of least resistance. If we stay in the channels, all is easy. To get out requires some extra drive, enthusiasm or energy.

This is in some degree a matter of sheerly physical energy. No matter how intellectual or spiritual one's interests may be, there is an immensely important physical element in one's capacity to learn, grow, recover from defeats, surmount obstacles and live life with vitality and resilience. Anyone interested in leading a creative life will have the deepest respect and concern for the marvelously intricate organism that so many of us take for granted.

But aside from staying in good health, is it really possible to do anything about one's own motivation? The answer is "Perhaps."

Everyone has noted the abundant resources of energy that seem available to those who enjoy what they are doing or find meaning in what they are doing. Self-renewing people know that if they have no great conviction about what they are doing they had better find something that they *can* have great conviction about. All of us cannot spend all of our time pursuing our deepest convictions. But all of us, either in our careers or as part-time activities, should be doing *something* about which we care deeply. If we are to escape the prison of the self, it must be something not essentially egocentric in nature.

How many times have we seen people leave work that they care deeply about to do something that does not interest them because it will bring more money or higher status or greater power? How many times have we seen middle-aged people caught in a pattern of activities they don't care about at all—playing bridge with people they don't really like, going to cocktail parties that bore them, doing things because "it's the thing to do." Such people would be refreshed and renewed if they could wipe the slate clean and do *one little thing* that they really cared about deeply, one little thing that they could do with burning conviction.

The conventions and artificialities of life, to say nothing of habit, routine and simple momentum, carry us so far from the sources of our interest and conviction that we all need a few primer lessons in how to get back in tune with our own being.

When Emerson said, "Once we had wooden chalices and golden priests; now we have golden chalices and wooden priests," he was saying something fundamental about the relation of humans to institutions.[10] We are forever "building the church and killing the creed." Form triumphs over spirit. A social institution is created out of human ardor and conviction. As its assets expand, the ardor wanes. The buildings grow bigger and the spirit thins out.[11]

Institutions are renewed by individuals who refuse to be satisfied with the outer husks of things. And self-renewal requires somewhat the same impatience with empty forms.

Those who want to get back to the source of their own vitality cut through the false fronts of life and seek out the things that they really believe in and can put their hearts into.

In this, self-renewing people remember the mythical giant, Antaeus, who was invincible in wrestling as long as he remained in contact with the earth. He is worth recalling in our intricately organized, ververbalized civilization. We drift further and further from the realities of life. Words become more real than the things they signify. The powerful factors in our lives become less and less things that can be touched and felt, more and more statistical indices and verbal abstractions. It is wisdom to cut through such abstractions and artificialities in a periodic return to the solid earth of direct experience.

Of course, one can overdo the business of complaining about the artificialities of our civilization. A symphony orchestra is as artificial as television. Penicillin is as artificial as neon lights. Most of the artificialities are designed to serve us in some important way. But if we are wise we turn our backs on them occasionally and seek to renew ourselves with the things we can see, hear and feel—direct contact with nature, face-to-face relations with our fellow beings, fashioning something with our own hands.

Some people think of motivation as a rather mysterious ingredient (initiative, ambition, the will to win) that is put into individuals to make them run, as gasoline is put into a car. Naturally, they are immensely curious as to the nature of that mysterious ingredient and eager to get more of it— particularly when they think the social tank is leaking, as they do today.

But motivation isn't a fuel that gets injected into the system. It is an attribute of individuals, in part linked to their physical vitality, in part a resultant of social forces— patterns of child-rearing, the tone of the educational system, presence or absence of opportunity, the tendency of the society to release or smother available energy, social attitudes toward dedication or commitment and the vitality of the society's shared values.[12]

In our own society the most popular explanation for lowered motivation is "too much prosperity." There is something to be said for the diagnosis. The old boxing adage that a hungry fighter is hard to beat is not without basis. And it is true that most individuals (and societies) deeply committed to the accomplishment of vital purposes are characterized by a certain austerity. But poverty doesn't always bring high motivation; some of the most impoverished populations in the world are the most lethargic. And prosperity doesn't always dampen motivation; indeed, a prosperous society—by virtue of its capacity to extend the range of individual opportunity—may release energies which would otherwise have lain dormant. Certain kinds of creativity require a reasonable margin of abundance. People under severe deprivation are not free to experiment and to try new ways of doing things. In all creative achievement there is a certain recklessness or gambling quality that is often suppressed in a society close to the margin of survival.

In short, although it pleases our puritanical streak to believe that prosperity has blunted our drive, the loss of motivation from this cause is greatly overestimated.

One may argue, as Toynbee does, that a society needs challenge. It is true. But no society has ever mastered its environment and itself to the extent that no challenge remained. Many have gone to sleep because they failed to understand the challenge that was undeniably there.[13] In a sense, societies create their own challenges.

David McClelland makes an interesting case for the view that child-rearing practices determine the level of motivation in a society.[14] We don't know enough to say with confidence what kinds of child-rearing practices will contribute to high levels of motivation; but qualified experts believe that such an outcome will be favored if the family sets standards for the child's performance, encourages habits of self-reliance and avoids excesses of authoritarianism.

The relation of education to the level of motivation in the society is more direct than most people recognize. The goals the young person sets for himself are very heavily affected by the framework of expectations with which adults surround him. The educational system provides the young person with a sense of what society expects of him in the way of performance. If it is lax in its demands, then he will believe that such are the expectations of his society. If much is expected of him, the chances are that he will expect much of himself. This is why it is important that a society create an atmosphere that encourages effort, striving and vigorous performance. In its early days—when it is struggling upward—such effort is apt to be highly rewarded. As the society becomes more successful it often demands less in terms of vigorous effort.

CHAPTER 3

VERSATILITY

EDUCATING FOR RENEWAL

We are beginning to understand how to educate for renewal but we must deepen that understanding. If we indoctrinate the young person in an elaborate set of fixed beliefs, we are ensuring his early obsolescence. The alternative is to develop skills, attitudes, habits of mind and the kinds of knowledge and understanding that will be the instruments of continuous change and growth on the part of the young person. Then we will have fashioned *a system that provides for its own continuous renewal.*[1]

This suggests a standard in terms of which we may judge the effectiveness of all education—and so judged, much education today is monumentally ineffective. All too often we are giving our young people cut flowers when we should be teaching them to grow their own plants. We are stuffing their heads with the products of earlier innovation rather than teaching them to innovate. We think of the mind as a storehouse to be filled when we should be thinking of it as an instrument to be used.

Of course, our schools cannot be wholly preoccupied with educating for innovation; they are concerned with continuity as well as change. There are continuities in the human condition, continuities in our own tradition and lessons to be learned from the past. When young people learn what and who they are it helps them to think about what they wish to become—as individuals and as a people. At the higher levels of education they must be given the opportunity to examine critically the shared purposes of their society—a major element in continuity—and to subject these purposes to the reappraisal that gives them vitality and relevance. In every area in which creative thought or action may occur, the individual builds on the heritage of earlier work. It is true that excessive preoccupation with that heritage may diminish his creativity. And it is true that his mode of building on his heritage may be to rebel from it. Still it is his starting point.

But the educational system has always been *relatively* successful in dealing with continuity. The pressing need today is to educate for an accelerating rate of change. Some observers have feared that the need would lead the schools into frantic pursuit of the latest fads, but it has had the opposite effect. Change is so swift that the "latest thing" today may be old-fashioned by the time young people enter adulthood. So they must be taught in such a way that they can learn for themselves the new things of tomorrow. And that leads us back to fundamentals.

We are moving away from teaching things that readily become outmoded, and toward things that will have the greatest long-term effect on the young person's capacity to understand and perform. Increasing emphasis is being given to instruction in methods of analysis and modes of attack on problems. In many subjects this means more attention to basic principles, less to applications of immediate "practical" use. In all subjects it means teaching habits of mind that will be useful in new situations—curiosity, open-mindedness, objectivity, respect for evidence and the capacity to think critically.

GENERALISTS AND SPECIALISTS

Education for renewal is to a considerable degree education for versatility. And that fact brings us face-to-face with a well-worn controversy: should we be training specialists or generalists? Though many educators respond with vehement confidence, the question poses extremely complex issues.

Specialization is a universal feature of biological functioning, observable in the cell structure of any complex organism, in insect societies and in human social organization. In human societies, division of labor is older than recorded history and has flourished wherever urban civilization has existed.

Specialization involves selective emphasis on certain functions and the dropping of other functions. The human organism is capable of an unimaginably broad range of behavioral variations. Out of this vast range, any individual can develop only a small fraction of the total. All learning is specialization in the sense that it involves reinforcement of some responses rather than others. Nothing illustrates the process better than language learning. The infant has the capacity to understand and to produce a vast variety of speech sounds. Out of this variety he will come to recognize and to utter chiefly those sounds present in his own language —a fraction of the total—and will, as an adult, have considerable difficulty in recognizing and uttering sounds not in his own language. Thus we are all specialists despite ourselves. And so it has always been.

In short, specialization is biologically, socially and intellectually necessary. The highest reaches of education will always involve learning one thing in great depth. The great artist or scientist often achieves the heights of performance through intensive cultivation of a narrow sector of his potentialities.

Clearly, then, we cannot do away with specialization, nor would we wish to. But in the modern world it has extended far beyond anything we knew in the past. And, unfortunately, there are many tasks that can be effectively performed only by men and women who have retained some capacity to function as generalists—leadership and management, certain kinds of innovation, communication and teaching and many of the responsibilities of child-rearing and of citizenship. Furthermore, the extremely specialized man may lose the adaptability so essential in a changing world. He may be unable to reorient himself when technological changes make his speciality obsolete.

Note that it is not a question of doing away with the specialist. It is a question of retaining some capacity to function as a generalist, and the capacity to shift to new specialties as circumstances require.

All social hierarchies involve a kind of specialization, and this too results in losses as well as gains. Subordinates who are deprived of the opportunity to make certain kinds of decisions may lose the capacity to make those decisions. An ironic consequence of such hierarchical specialization is that the individual higher in the scale may lose more in functional capacity than those below him. No one is more helpless than the boss without his accustomed aides. A slave-owning class may experience a deterioration in capacity that is damaging to its own survival. This process has interesting parallels in insect societies. Among certain slaveholding formicine ants, many normal capacities (nest making, care of young, even the capacity to feed themselves) have literally disappeared, leaving only a hypertrophied "military" or slave-making competence.[2]

In human societies there is no reason whatever why specialists should not retain the capacity to function as generalists. Whether they actually do so depends partly on their motivation, partly on the manner in which they are educated and partly on the nature of the organization or society in which their abilities mature.

Frontier societies and organizations in early stages of development tend to be simple, fluid and uncompartmentalized, and this puts pressure on the individual to be functionally generalized. Thus the "universal man" has most commonly appeared in young and relatively unstructured societies or early in an era. (Recall the versatility of our Founding Fathers.)

In later stages, societies and organizations develop a complex division of labor, high specialization and a great deal of compartmentalization—all of which press the individual to specialize. Every student of organization can comment on the possible hazards of such compartmentalization. To the extent that it diminishes the versatility of the individual it lessens the capacity of the organization to renew itself. If individuals are rigidly specialized and unprepared for change, the human cost of change will be high and the society will resist it stubbornly. But if they are flexible and capable of learning new ways, the human cost of readjustment will be low and there will be little resistance to it. In short, in a world of change the versatile individual is a priceless asset.

Farsighted administrators often take specific steps to prevent excessive compartmentalization. They reorganize to break down calcified organizational lines. They shift personnel (perhaps even establish a system of rotation) to eliminate unnecessary specialization and to broaden perspectives. They redefine jobs to break them out of rigid categories.

A free society cannot be rearranged in any such summary fashion, and in the long run perhaps the most effective means of achieving comparable results is through the educational system. Education can lay a broad and firm base for a lifetime of learning and growth. Individuals who begin with such a broad base will always have some capacity to function as generalists, no matter how deeply they choose to specialize. Education at its best develops the inner resources of young people to the point where they can learn (and will want to learn) on their own. It equips them to cope with unforeseen challenges and to live as versatile men and women in an unpredictable world. Individuals so educated will keep the society itself flexible, adaptive and innovative.

CHAPTER 4

INNOVATION

SOMETHING NEW UNDER THE SUN

Lyman Bryson said, ". . . the purpose of a democratic society is to make great persons. . . .[1] A democratic way of doing anything is a way that best keeps and develops the intrinsic powers of men and women."[2]

The institutional arrangements of an open society are not themselves the means of renewal. Their virtue is that they nourish free individuals. And such people are inexhaustible sources of renewal. We may learn something about the renewal of societies if we look at the kind of people who contribute most to that outcome—the innovators. But first we must examine the process of innovation.

Some writers have emphasized that innovative activity starts with a problem to be solved. That is usually true. But humans are inquisitive, exploring creatures, who can't keep their restless minds inactive even when there is no problem to be solved. They cannot help poking at things, turning ideas over in their minds, trying new combinations, groping for new insights. Surely, from the beginning, many of the most significant advances have come from just such exploring by gifted minds. Everyone who has spent any time with scientists knows that the answer to the question "Why did you try that particular thing?" is not infrequently "I was just curious to see what would happen."

Innovation is sometimes dramatized as a powerfully disruptive force that shatters the *status quo*. And so it sometimes is. But undue emphasis on its disruptive character can be misleading. Historically, the *status quo* in human societies, primitive or civilized, has been threatened not by innovation but by ancient and familiar crises—failure of food supply, disease, the hostility of neighboring societies, competition from superior technologies, inner decay. In such cases effective innovation may increase the chances of survival of a threatened system. (Ironically, this fact that the innovator may come in the role of savior does not necessarily make him any more acceptable to those who love the *status quo*. Like children, they may fear the doctor more than the disease.)

Just as societies come to a point of crisis at which they must move on to new solutions or perish, so particular fields of activity reach such a point. Just as a population may exhaust its food supply, so artists may exhaust the potentialities of a particular art form and scholars may exhaust the possibilities of a given line of inquiry.

The image of innovation as the shatterer of a serene *status quo* is particularly inappropriate in the modern world. Today, in the tumultuous sweep of technological and social change, one would be hard put to find any placid *status quo*. The solutions of today will be out of date tomorrow. The system that is in equilibrium today will be thrown off balance tomorrow. Innovation is continuously needed to cope with such altered circumstances.

Today even the most potent innovators are unlikely to be effective unless their work coincides with a crisis or series of crises that put people in a mood to accept innovation. The Paul Revere story is a very inadequate guide to action in a complex modern society. It was all too wonderfully simple. He saw danger, he sounded the alarm, and people really did wake up. In a big, busy society the modern Paul Revere is not even heard in the hubbub of voices. When he sounds the alarm no one answers. If he persists, people put him down as a controversial character. Then some day an incident occurs that confirms his warnings. The citizen who had refused to listen to the warnings now rushes to the window, puts his head out, nightcap and all, and cries, "Why doesn't somebody tell me these things?"

At that point the citizen is ready to support some new solutions, and wise innovators will take advantage of that fact. A man working on a new air-traffic control technique said recently, "I haven't perfected it yet, but it wouldn't be accepted today anyway because people aren't worried enough. Within the next two years there will be another spectacular air disaster that will focus the public mind on this problem. That will be my deadline and my opportunity."

The reader will assume, of course, that he is not the nightcapped citizen mentioned above. It is an unsafe assumption. How many of us can really recognize in the vast clutter of modern life the seedlings of new ideas and new ways that will shape the future? The new thing rarely comes on with a flourish of trumpets. The historic innovation looks exciting in the history books, but if one could question those who lived at the time, the typical response would be neither "I opposed it" nor "I welcomed it," but "I didn't know it was happening."

The capacity of public somnolence to retard change illuminates the role of the critic. In the early years of this century Abraham Flexner touched off a revolution in medical education by placing before the public a brilliant exposé of existing medical schools. Critics who call attention to an area that requires renewal are very much a part of the innovative process. (Of course, all critics are not heralds of the new. Some are elegant connoisseurs of that which has arrived, and when they approve of something it is likely to be long past its creative period. Like Hermes conducting the souls of the dead to Hades, they usher ideas and art forms into the mausoleums of "the accepted.")

One of the most serious obstacles to clear thinking about renewal is the excessively narrow conception of the innovator that is commonly held. It focuses on technology and on the persons who invent specific new devices: Alexander Graham Bell and the telephone; Marconi and wireless; Edison and the phonograph; the Wright Brothers and the airplane. Starting from this narrow view, we would not find it easy to accept Jakob Fugger, the Renaissance merchant prince, as an innovator, yet he deserves the label. Claudio Monteverdi was functioning as an innovator when he modified and synthesized a number of musical traditions to create Italian opera. Several of our Founding Fathers were impressive innovators in statecraft. Dorothea Dix was an immensely effective innovator in social welfare.

We tend to think of innovators as those who contribute to a new way of doing things. But many far-reaching changes have been touched off by those who contributed to a new way of thinking about things. Thus did Planck, Einstein and Rutherford end the Newtonian era and usher in modern physics. Thus did Socrates, Zeno of Citium, St. Augustine,

Copernicus and Darwin alter the course of intellectual history. One cannot reflect on such names without recognizing how striking is the diversity in content and style of innovation.

It would be a mistake to distinguish too sharply between those who contribute a new way of doing and those who contribute a new way of thinking. Many do both. As Hippocrates taught his contemporaries a new way to practice medicine, he taught them a new way of thinking about medicine, a way that lifted it out of the context of magic and superstition. As Louis Sullivan introduced a new way of building, he introduced a new way of thinking about building.

But we shall never fully comprehend the process of renewal if we limit our attention to the most spectacular historical figures. Many of the major changes in history have come about through successive small innovations, most of them anonymous. Our dramatic sense (or our superficiality) leads us to seek out the person "who started it all" and to heap on his or her shoulders the whole credit for a prolonged, diffuse and infinitely complex process.

It is essential that we outgrow this immature conception. Some of our most difficult problems today are such as to defy correction by any single dramatic solution. They will yield, if at all, only to a whole series of innovations. An example may be found in the renewal of our metropolitan areas. To bring these sprawling giants back under the rational control of the people who live in them will require a prolonged burst of political, economic and social innovation.

CREATIVITY

When we speak of the individual as a source of renewal, we call to mind the magic word *creativity*—a word of dizzying popularity at the moment. It is more than a word today; it is an incantation. People think of it as a kind of psychic wonder drug, powerful and presumably painless; and everyone wants a prescription.

It is one of our national vices to corrupt and vulgarize any word or idea that seems to have significance or relevance or freshness. And so we have done with the word *creativity*. But that should not lead us to neglect the idea behind the word. Granted that much of the current interest in the subject is shallow. Still it is more than a fad. It is part of a growing resistance to the tyranny of the formula, a new respect for individuality, a dawning recognition of the potentialities of the liberated mind.

We must never forget that though the word may be popular the consequences of true creativity can never be assured of popularity. New ways threaten the old, and those who are wedded to the old may prove highly intolerant. Today Galileo is a popular historical figure, and we feel wise and emancipated as we reflect indignantly on his persecution for supporting Copernicus. But if he were to reappear today and assert something equally at odds with *our own* deepest beliefs, his popularity would plummet like one of those lead weights dropped from the Tower of Pisa. Our affection is generally reserved for innovators long dead.

Even Pasteur, who enjoyed as much acclaim in his lifetime as any innovator who ever lived, was the object—all his life —of bitter attack and opposition. And he understood that it was inevitable.

One day, when I was a candidate for a vacant seat at the Academy of Sciences . . . one of the oldest and most dignified members said to me . . . "My friend, if they stop speaking disparagingly of you in certain journals, tell yourself that you are slipping."[3]

That is why innovative people often need protection. That is why a strong tradition of freedom of thought and inquiry is essential to continuous renewal.

People are not divided into two categories, those who are creative and those who are not.[4] There are degrees of the attribute. Rare are the individuals who have it in their power to achieve the highest reaches of creativity. But many can and do achieve fairly impressive levels of creativity under favorable circumstances. And quite a high proportion of the population could show *some* creativity *some* of the time in *some* aspect of their lives.

Popular and scientific opinion agree that the trait we are discussing is something more than intelligence alone. Each of us knows at least one brilliant individual who is essentially no more original or innovative than one of the more accomplished computers. Extensive research has demonstrated that the standardized tests of intelligence are not effective in identifying creative individuals.

Similarly, creativity requires mastery of the medium in which the work is to be done, but is something more than sheer mastery. The great artist, writer, scientist or architect has first of all mastered his craft—mastered it to the point where one might almost say that he can forget it. But all masters of a craft are not creative. The average scientist, author, artist or musician may be a solid craftsman, admirable in many ways, but not necessarily gifted with originality. In science one finds a relatively thin line of innovative individuals working at the frontier of discovery, and behind them a vast army of competent people doing routine work.

Creativity is possible in most forms of human activity. In some activities—bricklaying, let us say—the possibility is greatly limited by the nature of the task. The highest levels can be expected where performance is not severely constricted by the nature of the task to be accomplished, and in those lines of endeavor that involve man's emotions, judgment, symbolizing powers, aesthethic perceptions and spiritual impulses.

The creative process is often not responsive to conscious efforts to initiate or control it. It does not proceed methodically or in programmatic fashion. It meanders. It is unpredictable, digressive, capricious. As one scientist put it, "I can schedule my lab hours, but I can't schedule my best ideas." Obviously in any complex performance the process must at some point be brought under conscious discipline and control. But the role of the unconscious mind in creative work is clearly substantial.

Is it possible to foster creativity? The question is not easily answered. Popular books on the subject seem to be saying that the trait in question is like a muscle that profits from exercise (and the implication is that you too can bulge in the right places). Or they may take the line that creativity is a communicable secret like a golf grip or a good recipe. But research workers believe that this trait and the qualities of character, temperament and intellect that contribute to it are laid down in childhood and depend to a considerable degree on relationships within the family. We know too little about these early influences.

As far as adults are concerned, it is not certain whether anything can be done to supply creativity that is not already present. But much can be done to release the potential that is there. It is the almost universal testimony of people who possess this trait that certain kinds of environment smother their creative impulses and other kinds permit the release of these impulses.[5] The society interested in continuous renewal will strive to be a hospitable environment for the release of creativity.

When Alexander the Great visited Diogenes and asked whether he could do anything for the famed teacher, Diogenes replied, "Only stand out of my light." Perhaps some day we shall know how to heighten creativity. Until then, one of the best things we can do for creative men and women is to stand out of their light.

There are many kinds of creative individuals. Creative writers are distinguishable from creative mathematicians, and both are distinguishable from creative architects. Yet research suggests that there are traits which are shared by all of these and by most other highly original people.[6]

Openness. In studies of creative people one finds many references to a quality that might be described as "openness." At one level, openness refers to the receptivity of individuals to the sights, sounds, events and ideas that impinge on them. Most of us are skillful in shutting out the world, and what we do observe we see with a jaded eye. Men or women with the gift of originality manage to keep a freshness of perception, an unspoiled awareness.

Of course this openness to experience is limited to those features of the external world that seem to individuals to be relevant to their inner lives. No one could be indiscriminately open to all the clutter and clatter of life. Creative individuals achieve their heightened awareness of some aspects of life by ignoring other aspects. And since the aspects they ignore are often precisely those conventional matters on which the rest of us lavish loving attention, they are often put down as odd.

More significant than their receptivity to the external world is their exceptional openness to their own inner life. They do not suppress or refuse to face their own emotions, anxieties and fantasies. In more technical terms, MacKinnon and his associates say that creative persons are better able "to relinquish conscious control and to face without fear and anxiety the impulses and imagery arising from more primitive and unconscious layers of the personality."[7] They have fewer internal barriers or watertight compartments of experience. They are self-understanding, self-accepting.

The significance of this openness to one's own inner experience is obvious in the case of creative writers. As a result of it, they have access to the full richness of one person's emotional, spiritual and intellectual experience. But the trait can be relevant even in the cases of people who appear to be dealing wholly with the external world. Creative engineers let their hunches and wild ideas come to the surface, where the uncreative ones would tend to censor them.

Independence. Creative individuals have the capacity to free themselves from the web of social pressures in which the rest of us are caught. They don't spend much time asking "What will people say?" The fact that "everybody's doing it" doesn't mean they're doing it. They question assumptions that the rest of us accept. As J. P. Guilford has pointed out, they are particularly gifted in seeing the gap between what *is* and what *could be* (which means, of course, that they have achieved a certain measure of detachment from what *is*).[8]

It is easy to fall into romantic exaggeration in speaking of the capacity of people of originality to stand apart. Those who are responsible for the great innovative performances have always built on the work of others, and have enjoyed many kinds of social support, stimulation and communication. They are independent but they are not adrift.

The independence or detachment of creative individuals is at the heart of their capacity to take risks and to expose themselves to the probability of criticism from their fellows. Does this mean that they are nonconformists? Yes, but not necessarily in the popular sense of the word. One of the interesting findings contained in recent research is that creative individuals as a rule choose to conform in the routine, everyday matters of life, such as speech, dress and manners. One gets the impression that they are simply not prepared to waste their energy in nonconformity about trifles. They reserve their independence for what really concerns them— the area in which their creative activities occur. This distinguishes them sharply from the exhibitionists who reject convention in those matters that will gain the most attention.

Flexibility. Still another widely observed trait may be labeled flexibility. It is perhaps best seen in what has been called the playfulness of persons of originality. They will toy with an idea, "try it on for size," look at it from a dozen different angles, argue to themselves that it is true and then argue that it is untrue. Unlike the rest of us, they do not persist stubbornly in one approach to a problem. They can change directions and shift strategies. They can give up their initial perception of a problem and redefine it.

An even more important ingredient in their flexibility is their capacity to maintain a certain detachment from the conventional categories and abstractions that people use, and a similar detachment from the routines and fixed customs of those around them. They even manage to exercise a reasonable detachment from their own past attitudes and habits of mind, their own pet categories. (In the current fashion we talk much of the limitations on freedom that result from outside pressures and tend to forget the limitations imposed by one's own compulsions, neuroticisms, habits and fixed ideas.)

Related to this flexibility is a trait of the creative person that psychologists have called a "tolerance for ambiguity." These individuals have a capacity to tolerate internal conflict, a willingness to suspend judgment. They are not uncomfortable in the presence of unanswered questions or unresolved differences. They do not find it difficult to give expression to opposite sides of their nature at the same time—conscious and unconscious mind, reason and passion, aesthetic and scientific impulses.

Some observers have been led to comment on a certain "childlike" or "primitive" quality in creative individuals. They *are* childlike and primitive in the sense that they have not been trapped by the learned rigidities that immobilize the rest of us. In their chosen field they do not have the brittle knowingness and sophistication of people who think they know all the answers. The advantage of this fluidity is that it permits all kinds of combinations and recombinations of experience with a minimum of rigidity.

Capacity to Find Order in Experience. The individual of high originality, having opened himself to such a rich and varied range of experience, exhibits an extraordinary capacity to find the order that underlies that varied experience, I would even say an extraordinary capacity to *impose* order on experience. And, as MacKinnon has suggested, it may be that the creative individual could not tolerate such a wild profusion of ideas and experiences if he did not have profound confidence in his capacity to bring some new kind of order out of this chaos.

This aspect of the creative process has not received the emphasis it deserves. We have made much of the fact that innovators free themselves from the old patterns and have neglected to emphasize that they do so in order to forge new patterns. This, if you reflect on it, suggests a picture of the creative individual fundamentally different from the romanticized version. The portraits in popular literature of artists or other creative persons have all too frequently led us to suppose that people of high originality are somehow lawless. The truly creative person is not an outlaw but a lawmaker. Every great creative performance since the initial one has been in some measure a bringing of order out of chaos. It brings about a new relatedness, connects things that did not previously seem connected, sketches a more embracing framework, moves toward larger and more inclusive understandings.

One could list a number of other traits that have been ascribed to the creative individual by research workers. Almost all observers have noted a remarkable zeal or drive in creative individuals. They are wholly absorbed in their work. Anne Roe, in her study of gifted scientists, found that one of their most striking traits was a willingness to work hard and for long hours.[9] The energy they bring to their work is not only intense but sustained. Most of the great creative performances grow out of years of arduous application.

Other observers have commented on the confidence, self-assertiveness or, as one investigator put it, the "sense of destiny" in creative persons. They have faith in their capacity to do the things they want and need to do in the area of their chosen work.

THE REVOLUTIONARY

One might imagine that revolutionaries would bear some resemblance to creative persons, but they are distinctly different kinds of people. Some revolutionaries are in themselves (that is, in their personality structure) not even slightly creative: circumstances thrust them into the role of opponents of the *status quo* and make them instruments of change, but they themselves may be more rigid and uncreative than the forces they are opposing. Stalin may have been such a man. Other revolutionaries may enjoy a creative phase in their lives only to leave it behind as their characters harden in the heat of battle. Still others may remain creative to the end.

As radicals move into the conflict that is often required to produce social change they tend to rigidify as individuals and to form themselves into highly dogmatic organizations, intolerant of diversity within their own ranks. It is because of this fierce intolerance of internal diversity that reformist movements commonly splinter. They splinter because there is no reasonable way to disagree except by breaking up. This is equally true whether we are speaking of radicals of the left or radicals of the right. It is a consequence of extremism, not of substantive philosophy.

It is for these reasons that the revolutionary will be forever at odds with the "normal" people in the world. The normal American Christian churchgoer, no matter how devout, would be acutely uncomfortable, not to say alarmed, if he were to have some of the Early Christians as house guests. The American Protestant today would experience intense uneasiness if he were thrown into close association with some of the leaders of the Reformation. Most of us approve the results of the suffragist movement and admire the doughty women who led it, but their sheer intensity troubled their contemporaries. Why did they have to be so terribly fierce about it?

The answer is that people who break the iron frame of custom are necessarily people of ardor and aggressiveness. They are capable of pursuing their objectives with fervor and singleness of purpose. If they were not, they would not succeed. And it is sad but true that in shaping themselves into bludgeons with which to assault the social structure they often develop a diamond-hard rigidity of their own. Thus arises the familiar problem of what to do with the revolutionaries when the revolution is over.

Modern art may be taken as an example of a major change in tastes, attitudes and practices that could not have been brought about without great emotional conviction and zeal. The fetters of convention and "the expected" in art were so powerful that the only way to break them was to break them intemperately and fiercely. It was necessary that the men who broke them feel very strongly on the subject. It was necessary that they be prepared to face ridicule. It was necessary that they act vehemently in behalf of their views. When such things become necessary, no one knows what the end will be. The word *revolution* has a favorable connotation for most liberals, partly because the picture in their heads is of a nicely regulated revolution run by reasonably housebroken revolutionists. In real life, the revolution one ends up with is rarely the same revolution one started with. The intensity of emotion and shock of battle may produce unexpected results. In this case the revolution in modern art succeeded magnificently in shattering the rigidities of traditional art. It also fastened on the field of painting a mystique of rebellion and innovation which has hung around its neck like an albatross ever since.

CHAPTER 5

OBSTACLES TO RENEWAL

MIND-FORGED MANACLES

To achieve renewal we need to understand what prevents renewal. And most of the things that prevent it are to be found in the mind rather than in external arrangements. As every good management consultant knows, it is relatively easy to specify the things about an organization that need renewal; what is difficult is to cope with the habits and attitudes that permitted the organization to go to seed in the first place. Similarly, the economist has learned that after he has diagnosed the economic problems of an underdeveloped society he must cope with the habits, attitudes and belief systems that prevent economic growth.

When we talk about revitalizing a society or an organization we tend to put exclusive emphasis on finding new ideas. But there is usually no shortage of new ideas; the problem is to get a hearing for them. And that means breaking through the crusty rigidity and stubborn complacency of the *status quo*. The aging society or organization has developed defenses against new ideas—"mind-forged manacles," in William Blake's vivid phrase.

So stubborn are the defenses of a mature society against change that shock treatment is often required to bring about renewal. A nation will postpone critically important social changes until war or depression forces the issue. Many a business firm has had to go through bankruptcy before initiating obviously necessary reforms.

It is a grisly fact that catastrophes often produce significant regeneration. Santa Barbara, one of the handsomest cities on the Pacific coast, owes much of its civic beauty to the fact that it was almost totally destroyed by an earthquake in 1925; the widespread destruction gave the city fathers the priceless opportunity to rebuild intelligently.[1] It is a sad commentary on the modern metropolis that there have been few catastrophes in our great cities that have not left a net gain of beauty.

As we have already noted in Chapter 2, similar explosive force is often required to bring about substantial changes in individual beliefs, attitudes, customs or procedures once they have become hardened.[2]

How does a society develop such stubborn resistance to innovation? In some respects it is not unlike the process of individual narrowing which we have already discussed. The new organization is loose in procedure, unclear in organizational lines, variable in policies. It is willing to experiment with a variety of ways to solve its problems. It is not bound by the weight of tradition. It rushes in where angels fear to tread.

As it matures it develops settled ways of doing things and becomes more orderly, more efficient, more systematic. But it also becomes less flexible, less innovative, less willing to look freshly at each day's experience. Its increasingly fixed routines are congealed in an elaborate body of written rules. In the final stage of organizational senility there is a rule or precedent for everything. Someone has said that the last act of a dying organization is to get out a new and enlarged edition of the rule book.[3]

Written rules are the least of the problem. More perplexing is the straitjacket of unwritten rules that hems the individual in. Some of these may represent attitudes and values that are among the most precious assets the organization possesses, e.g., standards of excellence, respect for the individual, shared purposes and high morale. But not all of the traditional ways in an organization are so constructive. In most societies and organizations there grows up a choking underbrush of customs and precedent. There comes to be an accepted way to do everything. Eccentric experimentation and radical departures from past practices are ruled out. The old hand says, "You just have to understand how we do things around here," and what he means is that "how we do things" is Sound and Respectable and The Best Way. Sir Henry Bessemer, inventor of the Bessemer process for steelmaking, said:

> I had an immense advantage over many others dealing with the problem inasmuch as I had no fixed ideas derived from long established practice to control and bias my mind, and did not suffer from the general belief that whatever is, is right.[4]

The body of custom and "reputable" standards exercises such an oppressive effect on creative minds that new developments often originate outside the area of respectable practice. The break with traditional art was not fostered within the Academy. Jazz did not spring from the bosom of the respectable music world. The land-grant college, a profoundly important educational innovation, did not spring from the inner circle of respectable higher education as it then existed—it represented an impulse from outside that charmed circle. Motels, the most significant development of this generation in innkeeping, were at first regarded with scorn by reputable hotel people.

Against this background we may re-examine with profit some of Frederick Jackson Turner's comments on the frontier experience:

> For a moment, at the frontier, the bonds of custom are broken and unrestraint is triumphant . . . each frontier did indeed furnish a new field of opportunity, a gate of escape from the bondage of the past; and freshness, and confidence, and scorn of older society, impatience of its restraints and its ideas, and indifference to its lessons, have accompanied the frontier. What the Mediterranean Sea was to the Greeks, breaking the bond of custom, offering new experiences, calling out new institutions and activities, that, and more, the ever-retreating frontier has been to the United States.[5]

A mature society must make a particular effort to reward its innovators, because its very maturity discourages innovation. Where there is an established way to do almost everything, people are apt to feel that all the pioneering has been done, all the exciting things tried.[6] Though the need for innovation still exists (or may even be greater), it is far from obvious. The challenge is not easily visible. In contrast, in the frontier situation the need is dramatic and universally understood. If the individual has a grain of capacity to improvise or innovate, the situation calls it forth.

With Chaucer and Shakespeare, English literature achieved heights of creativity that later centuries have not surpassed; and one sometimes hears expressions of wonder that such extraordinary achievements should have come so early in a long history. We are beginning to understand that those extravagant bursts of creativity may have come at least in part because of the earliness, not despite it.

Youth is characteristically impatient of carefully weighed procedures. The young organization (or individual) wants to "get to the point." The important thing is to get the job done and not to worry about how it is done. The emphasis is on serving the stark need as directly as possible with no frills.

But goals are achieved by some *means,* and sooner or later even the most impulsive man of action will discover that some ways of achieving the goal are more effective than others. A concern for *how* to do it is the root impulse in all great craftsmanship, and accounts for all of the style in human performance. Without it we would never know the peaks of human achievement.

Yet, ironically, this concern for "how it is done" is also one of the diseases of which societies die. Little by little, preoccupation with method, technique and procedure gains a subtle dominance over the whole process of goal seeking. *How* it is done becomes more important than *whether* it is done. Means triumph over ends. Form triumphs over spirit. Method is enthroned. Men become prisoners of their procedures, and organizations that were designed to achieve some goal become obstacles in the path to that goal.

A concern for "how to do it" is healthy and necessary. The fact that it often leads to an empty worship of method is just one of the dangers with which we have to live. Every human activity, no matter how ennobling or constructive or healthy, involves hazards. The flower of competence carries the seeds of rigidity just as the flower of virtue carries the seeds of complacency. "There is a road to hell," said John Bunyan, "even from the gates of heaven."[7]

One must not imagine that this is a disease of bureaucracies only. By a not dissimilar process artists often become prisoners of their style, and civilizations become prisoners of their greatest achievements.[8] As with Ahab, the thing that obsesses them finally destroys them.

As rules and customs proliferate, there is increasing emphasis on the appropriateness of one's behavior. The person who wins acclaim is not the one who is highly motivated nor the one who "gets things done" but the one who has an ingrained knowledge of the rules and traditional ways and a finely tuned sense of how to act in the light of those rules and traditions. Whether or not one actually accomplishes anything recedes in importance. In this stage, individuals lose confidence in their ability to function without the crutches provided by well-established operating rules.

One consequence of the proliferation of rules, customs and procedures is the bottling up of energy or, more accurately, the channeling of energy into all the tiny rivulets of conformity. The long process of mastering the rules smothers energy and destroys all zest, spontaneity or creativity. In the frontier situation, and in the young organization, without such stultifying forces at work there is an astonishing supply of free energy—energy to spare, energy to be extravagant with, energy unthwarted by intricate procedures, undissipated by red tape.

Thus we have an interesting contrast. The aging society or organization may have superb confidence in matters of procedure, technique and style but serious doubts concerning its ability to win. In contrast, the society or organization that is young, inexperienced and full of undisciplined energy may have great confidence in its vigor, drive and fitness to win, but a sense of inferiority about procedures, manners and style. The representatives of the vigorous new thing that is driving out the old are apt to appear deficient in style, sophistication and the many-layered, richly patterned, intricately figured culture that they are replacing.

A common stratagem of those who wish to escape the swirling currents of change is to stand on high moral ground. They assert that the old way is intimately bound up in moral and spiritual considerations that will be threatened by any change. When Russia in the eighteenth and nineteenth centuries had to face the superior technological development of Western Europe, Slavophiles were impelled to speak of the Russian soul, much as some writers in India today assert that the superiority of Western technology is more than balanced by India's spiritual depth. The new thing will usually look barbarous compared to the old. The era that is being born will often look less spiritual and less laden with the deeper values than the era that is dying. A society that has mastered the art of continuous renewal will not let such impressions distort its judgment. It will reject the notion that nothing is morally worthy unless it has been around for a long time.

It has been said that there is a stage in the life of a society (or organization or movement) in which the innovators and creative minds flower and a stage in which the connoisseurs and critics flower. Is it true that the heights of connoisseurship are achieved on the road to decadence? It is a highly debatable point, but not to be dismissed out of hand. Creative minds are rarely tidy.[9] New and dynamic movements commonly "overdo it." They do not find a sympathetic climate in that stage in which the supreme values are fastidious taste and discriminating judgment. And it must be admitted that education in its highest development leans naturally toward these latter. Thus there occurs the ironic situation in which parents who place a high value on creativity provide their children with education that nips that creativity in the bud by turning them into young connoisseurs.

Nothing is more familiar than the nostalgia which asserts that things were better in some past time ("the good old days," "the golden age"). Surely, at least in some measure, this is a rebellion against the increasing suppression of vitality by organization, by weight of custom and by the niceties and intricacies of a mature civilization.[10] People long for a time when impulse was not smothered by rules and dissipated in adherence to elaborate procedures. They long for a time when finely spun discriminations were unimportant and simple, uncomplicated values prevailed. They long for a time when the past was less of a burden, as did Hawthorne after a visit to the British Museum:

> I wandered from hall to hall with a weary and heavy heart, wishing (Heaven forgive me!) that the Elgin Marbles and the frieze of the Parthenon were all burnt to lime. . . . The present is burthened too much with the past. We have not time, in our earthly existence, to appreciate what is warm with life, and immediately around us; yet we heap up all these old shells, out of which human life has long emerged, casting them off forever. I do not see how future ages are to stagger onward under all this dead weight, with the additions that will be continually made to it.[11]

But nostalgia for an older, simpler time has always been a source of grave delusions about society and history. A primitive society may have a far more rigid structure of rules and customs than most modern men have experienced. Life in the Massachusetts Bay Colony in the late seventeenth century involved a substantially more oppressive structure of rules and precedents than most Americans have to put up with today.

This should give us heart. It suggests that communities that have rigidified may later break out of their rigidities and that a society such as ours is not subject to an irreversible process of aging. As a matter of fact, there is ample evidence of corrective mechanisms in a healthy society. Whether in art, in manners or in social structure, the trend to intricate elaboration often falls of its own weight, and people again seek a simple relationship to life and to one another.

VESTED INTERESTS

Of the processes that reduce the initial flexibility and venturesomeness of individuals and organizations, none is more celebrated in folk wisdom than the changes resulting from accumulation of possessions. Preoccupation with conserving what we have may make us much less venturesome than the individual who through choice or necessity is "traveling light." To some extent we are all owned by our possessions. As William James put it, "Lives based on having are less free than lives based either on doing or on being."[12]

It is not simply a question of possessions but of obligations of all sorts. The individual acquires debts, installment and insurance payments. Organizations acquire a heavy overhead and long-term commitments. An institution acquires an elaborate physical plant that cannot be easily disposed of or reshaped.

The accumulations that weigh one down may even be of

the nonmaterial sort, for example, reputation or status. An organization may avoid experimental ventures because it fears to damage its reputation for soundness. Many a gifted scholar has allowed his creative talent to be smothered by a growing commitment to his own previously stated doctrines. Many an established specialist fears the loss of his reputation if he ventures beyond the territory where he has proved his mastery. Indeed this fear is the greatest obstacle to intellectual breadth in the scholarly world.

Since no one wants to go back to having "nothing to lose," it is comforting to note that none of these consequences are inevitable. It is not so much a question of possessions as of the attitude one takes toward them. If affluent individuals (or the affluent society) commit themselves unreservedly to the conservation of their resources, affluence can be a deadening force. But if they regard their resources as providing a wide margin within which they can enjoy the luxury of creative experimentation with their environment, affluence can be a blessing. Individuals and societies living close to the margin of survival often cannot afford to take the chances required by innovative action.

In the case of an organization, much depends on the nature of the assets and commitments. Every manager of a large-scale enterprise knows the difference between the kinds of organizational commitment that limit freedom of action and the kinds that permit flexibility and easy changes of direction. But few understand how essential that flexibility is for continuous renewal. Assets committed to the goal of continuous renewal will never be a burden.

Vested interests constitute another problem for the aging society. The phrase has been associated chiefly with wealth and power; but, as all students of corporate organization know, the vested interests of the workers may be as strong as those of the top executives. Vested interests may be found wherever a man acquires a shirt for his back or rights and privileges he would be reluctant to lose. In any organization many of the established ways of doing things are held in place not by logic nor even by habit but by the force of one powerful consideration: changing them would jeopardize the rights, privileges or advantages of specific individuals —perhaps the president, perhaps the maintenance workers.

As individuals develop vested interests, the organization itself rigidifies. And a democratic form of organization is by no means immune to this consequence. Indeed, the more democratic it is the more vividly the vested interests of its members will be reflected in the policy of the organization. Thus a stagnant democratic organization may be particularly resistant to change.

In colleges and universities many of the regulations regarding required courses which are defended on highly intellectual grounds are also powerfully buttressed by the career interests of the faculty members involved in those courses. The building codes of most communities contain provisions that were inserted to protect the special position of one or another element in the community—building and supply companies, real estate operators and the like. In the labor movement make-work rules, featherbedding, excessively strict seniority provisions and the closed shop all represent arrangements that are the crystallization of vested interests.

It is not my purpose here to make the point that such vested interests exist: that point has frequently been made. It is my purpose to point out that they are among the most powerful forces producing rigidity and diminishing capacity for change. And these are the diseases of which organizations and societies die.

CHAPTER 6

TYRANNY WITHOUT A TYRANT

THE TYRANNY OF THE FORMULA

The tides of change that move society on to new solutions or catastrophes run deeper than the swirling events of the day. In relation to these great tidal movements, the trends we observe in our lifetimes are surface currents and the crises of the morning newspaper the merest whitecaps.

One of the deep tidal currents—perhaps the most fateful —is the movement over recent centuries toward the creation of ever larger, more complex and more highly organized social groupings.

It is a trend that we must examine here because it threatens the freedom and integrity of the individual; and the capacity of society for continuous renewal depends ultimately upon the individual. He is the seedbed of change, the inventor and innovator, the critic of old ways and mapper of new paths. John Stuart Mill wrote, "A state which dwarfs its men . . . will find that with small men no great thing can be accomplished."[1] We need only add that no *new* thing can be accomplished, no renewing thing, no revitalizing thing.

Ignorance, disease, undernourishment, political and economic subjugation are still the most powerful forces stunting
individual growth. But every thoughtful person today worries
about novel and subtle restraints placed on the individual
by modern large-scale organization—and fears that we may
triumph over the old evils only to find ourselves enmeshed
in a new and streamlined tyranny.

It is futile to hope that the movement toward more intricate and inclusive social organization will reverse itself. A
modern society is—and must be—characterized by complex
organization. It is not a matter of choice. We must cope as
best we can with the pressures that modern large-scale organization places on the individual. These pressures have
been a favorite theme of social critics and it is not necessary
to describe them here. But it may be useful to clear up some
of the confusions that have surrounded the subject.

One shortcoming in current writing on this subject has
been the tendency to seek a villain. An essential feature of
the individual's predicament today is that there is no villain.
It is not a question of one social class dominating another;
nor of believers in one dogma oppressing believers in another
dogma. It is not a tyrant who subjugates the individual. It is
not even that tired old bogeyman, Madison Avenue. Nor that
fanciful new bogeyman—The Establishment. What is oppressing the individual is the very nature of modern society.

Yet the search for a villain continues. Clearly, it fills some
emotional need on the part of the searchers.

There are oppressors on the scene, of course, and we may
learn something by observing them closely. We still think of
the typical dictator as one who flouts the wishes of the people,
but outright tyranny without concern for the appearance of
popular consent is the most old-fashioned of political ma-
neuvers today. The truly modern dictator achieves his goals

through the people, not in spite of them. He rides their aspirations to power. He manipulates their hopes and fears and is ushered into office with their joyous shouts. He may then construct, with the consent of the people, precisely the same machinery of control that he would otherwise have had to construct over their opposition. The process may be observed in some nations today, in some communities and in some labor unions.

If we understand how these things can happen, then we are in a position to understand that people can construct their own tyrannies. If one's freedom must be invaded, it is perhaps comforting to find the invasion accomplished democratically. But loss of freedom is loss of freedom.

Finally, as we have already seen, many threats to individual freedom do not stem even remotely from the relationships of authority and subordination nor indeed from any political circumstance, but from customs, traditions and conceptions of what is "proper procedure." These can be as coercive as any tyranny.

Another familiar error is to assume that the pressure on the individual may be understood as a liberal versus conservative issue or a government versus private enterprise issue. Nothing could be more misleading. Politically conservative men who saw themselves as rugged individualists created the modern corporation—a perfect example of the large-scale social organization that poses problems for the individual. Liberal-minded men who would count themselves devoted friends of freedom spearheaded the trend toward Big Government and Big Labor, both of which pose far-reaching problems for the individual.

The truth is that neither conservatives nor liberals are responsible for the hazards facing the modern individual.

Neither "creeping socialism" nor "the acquisitive society" is responsible. Modern mass society has developed under various ideological climates. The techniques of large-scale organization are not the property of any ideological group. The huge urban centers characteristic of mass society have developed with equal rapidity in Japan, India, Russia and the United States.

Still another error is to assert, as many do, that the "inhuman" aspects of modern social organization are the fault of science and technology. This view has deep emotional roots and there is not much point in arguing with those who hold it. They would rather stay mad.

But the truth is that workers in the grimmest moments of modern industrialism were no more miserable than, let us say, the Egyptian slaves who built the pyramids. It is not advanced technology that causes the trouble. The root of the difficulty is an attitude of mind that has never really died out in the world, nor perhaps even diminished greatly since the days of the Pharaohs—a willingness to sacrifice human values to other objectives.

Modern technology *need not* destroy aesthetic, spiritual and social values, but it will most certainly do so unless the individuals who manage our technology are firmly committed to the preservation of such values.

The tyranny of mass society is not a matter of one man's foot on another man's neck. It is a tyranny of the formula. Mass society searches for common denominators. Sheer numbers make it impossible to take account of individual identity. Serving the mass market requires standardization. Popular culture becomes homogenized. Even political campaigns are planned by the market researcher.

The exacting requirements of a highly organized society lead to the development of ingenious and powerful management techniques—in communications, information processing, cost accounting, personnel and public relations. Such techniques are rarely designed by men who harbor conscious tyrannical purposes. But in the hands of men insensitive to the needs of the individual such techniques do all too often result in the "processing" of human beings.

The pressures that produce conformity are often misunderstood. The precisely interlocked processes of a complex modern society require a high degree of predictability of individual behavior. The individual conforms because it seems like the sensible way to keep the organization running smoothly. Eccentric convictions, unpopular views, unique styles of behavior get in the way. Personnel directors look for the man who will fit in. Parents say, "You want to be popular, don't you?" The Image Managers encourage the individual to fashion himself into a smooth coin, negotiable in any market. An occasional Kierkegaard may insist that "the crowd is untruth," but the man in the street takes a more practical view.[2]

The long-run hazard for a society that needs independent and creative men and women to ensure its continued vitality is clear. The very subtlety and blandness of the process adds to the danger.

Another difficulty (which we have already explored) is that the complex processes of modern society tend to force the individual into an excessively specialized role. To the extent that they do they deprive him of the wholeness, versatility and generalized competence that he should preserve at all costs. Not only does it become increasingly difficult for him to comprehend his relationship to the world about him, he has less time (or inclination) to explore this relationship as he whittles himself down to fit a slot in the intricate pattern.

One of the clearest dangers in modern society is that men and women will lose the experience of participating in meaningful decisions concerning their own life and work, that they will become cogs in the machine because they *feel like* cogs in the machine. All too often today they are inert components of the group, not participating in any significant way but simply being carried along like grains of sand in a bucket.

Malcolm Cowley, speaking of the Lost Generation, wrote:

> But the decay of society was psychologically equivalent to its progress: both were automatic processes that we ourselves could neither hasten nor retard. Society was something alien, which our own lives and writings could never affect; it was a sort of parlor car in which we rode, over smooth tracks, toward a destination we should never have chosen for ourselves.[3]

The disastrous consequences of such attitudes for the morale of a society are obvious. Without some grasp of the meaning of their relationship to the whole, it is not easy for individuals to retain a vivid sense of their own capacity to act as individuals, a sure sense of their own dignity and an awareness of their roles and responsibilities. They tend to accept the spectator role and to sink into passivity.

It is not easy for a modern, complex society to prevent such an outcome. The individual is fixed in a network of abstractions. Instead of working for a known boss, he is employed by a corporation. Instead of coping with a rival across the street, he copes with forces of the market. Instead of fashioning a product with his own hands, he shuffles papers, juggles figures or pushes buttons. He receives orders from people he has never met and makes recommendations without knowing those who will be affected by them. A well-known government official offered a poignant vignette of modern organizational life when he said: "What we sign we haven't written, and what we write someone else signs."

The classic criticism of the assembly line is that work has been so organized that the worker has few decisions to make and never experiences the consequences of those he does make. It is important to note that this is a consequence of the way the work has been organized and not an evil inherent in The Machine. Emotional attacks on mechanization usually miss the point. The fault is not with mechanization as such. A bucket brigade can be as frustrating as an assembly line. The fault lies in an assignment of functions that ignores the needs of the individual.

This is in some measure an inevitable consequence of large-scale modern organization. Economies of scale can be achieved by centralizing decisions, and the complex modern society has been incredibly ingenious in accomplishing such centralization. Countless schemes and devices, from prepared cake mixes to electronic computers, relieve the individual of the burden of decision. No wonder critics worry that we will become sodden, passive consumers of predigested offerings and mindless performers of pre-programmed tasks.

But then the individual, with some obscure instinct for his own survival, takes up a hobby in which decisions are still possible. The do-it-yourself movement deserves comment. When a manufacturer markets high-fidelity sound equipment that is designed to be sold in an unassembled state so that the customer can have the fun of assembling it, he is going counter to some of the most powerful currents of our time. Over the past century, industrial society has devoted untold ingenuity and skill to the objective of placing a fool-proof, prefabricated device in the hands of a supposedly passive and moronic consumer. Now a respectable fraction of those consumers turn out to have vagrant impulses that are not served by ingenuities of prefabrication. They want to exercise their hands and minds on concrete tasks. They want to puzzle over something, shape something, contribute their sweat to something. We have hardly begun to absorb the implications of that fact.

ORGANIZING FOR FREEDOM

Large-scale organization does not always diminish the individual's freedom—in some respects it enlarges it.

As a result of large-scale organization most of us enjoy freedoms that we could not hope to enjoy otherwise. Out of the vast and elaborately organized medical center come findings that free the individual from illnesses that have plagued mankind for centuries. The great urban university, which strikes some critics as little more than a factory, places within reach of millions of low-income workers the opportunity to surmount ignorance and stretch their horizons.

Those who move from a small town to a large city experience unaccustomed freedom. They not only escape the stultifying web of attitudes, expectations and censorship that characterize the small town, they find in the city more choices in every dimension—kinds of dwelling, consumer goods, entertainment, social companions, culture and work.

Of course this freedom is quickly taken for granted. When people see that their range of choice has been widened, they simply raise their aspirations with respect to freedom of choice. Instead of being grateful for new freedoms, they resent more sharply the remaining limits on their freedom. We must never forget that, while the modern world has produced grounds for complaint, it has also produced the person doing the complaining. The truth is we expect more than any of our forebears expected.

The point was brought home to me recently when I visited an academic friend. He sat in an air-conditioned study. Behind him was a high-fidelity phonograph and record library that brought him the choicest music of three centuries. On the desk before him was the microfilm of an ancient Egyptian papyrus that he had obtained by a routine request through his university library. He described a ten-day trip he had just taken to London, Paris and Cairo to confer on recent archaeological discoveries. In short, modern technology and social organization were serving him in spectacular ways. And what was he working on at the moment? An essay for a literary journal on the undiluted evil of modern technology and large-scale organization.

Some critics argue that the growth in size and complexity of organization has been accompanied by an increase in relationships of authority and subordination, but anthropologists and historians would not support this view. The spirit of hierarchy can flourish quite as fiercely in an organization consisting of one man and his secretary as it can in General Motors. Small businesses do not necessarily offer their employees a more equalitarian atmosphere than do large corporations. Small nations with a pre-modern social structure have managed to be quite as authoritarian as modern nations, generally more so. As a matter of fact, the primitive tribe or **preindustrial community has usually demanded far more profound submission of the individual to the group than has any modern society.**

In short, large-scale organization is not to be condemned out of hand. That is what makes the problem so difficult—and so interesting. Organization serves us and rules us, increases our scope and hems us in. We must be exceedingly discriminating in weighing its benefits against possible disadvantages. And in doing so we shall discover that everything depends on the patterns of organization.

We cannot return to a simpler world. Much of contemporary social criticism is made irrelevant by its refusal to face that fact. It is true that the pressure and tumult of our society compares unfavorably with, say, the tranquillity of a village in Brittany. But the comparison does not deal with a choice that is open to us. We must live in the modern world. We cannot stem the pressure for more intricate organization of our economy, our production, our social, political and cultural life. We must master the new forms of organization or they will master us.

The most hopeful thing today is that on *some fronts* we seem to be achieving patterns of organization that avoid the stultification, rigidity and threats to freedom inherent in monolithic integrations. If this is true, it may be the most important single fact in our future.

It is possible to continue achieving economies of scale and still give attention to human needs. Too often in the past we have designed systems to meet all kinds of exacting requirements except the requirement that they contribute to the fulfillment and growth of the participants. Organizations need not be designed in such a way that they destroy human initiative. They are designed that way because we have not been willing to be as inventive about organizational matters as we have been about hardware.

It is essential that in the years ahead we undertake intensive analysis of the impact of the organization on the individual. We must examine the conditions under which organization is a threat to the individual, the kinds of organizational patterns that are the greatest threat and the safeguards that can be built into organization to minimize the threat. We must discover how to design organizations and technological systems in such a way that individual talents are used to the maximum and human satisfaction and dignity preserved. We must learn to make technology serve us not only in the end product but in the doing.

Some of our social critics believe that the way to fight for freedom in a world of organization is to be, in so far as possible, a nonconforming curmudgeon. They would say, in Samuel Goldwyn's immortal phrase, "Include me out." This is not entirely to be deplored. We may see a time when we shall be grateful for individuals who are willing to shake their fists at an overorganized world. But as a strategy it has its limits. If one values freedom enough to fight for it intelligently, one will want to understand why and how certain factors in organizational life are detrimental to the individual and other factors are beneficial.

But knowledge is not enough. It never is. It could be used to enslave us as well as to liberate us. In truth, the considerable technical grasp of organization we now have has often been used in ways that are damaging to individual integrity. Knowledge will be a safe weapon *only* if it is linked to a deeply rooted conviction that organizations are made for humans and not humans for organizations.

The whole purpose of such knowledge is to design environments conducive to individual fulfillment. It is ridiculous that the institutions we design for our own benefit should work to our disadvantage. We can never eliminate the conflict between humans and their institutions, nor would we wish to, but we can insist that one of the aims of any organization be the development of the individuals who make it up.

We shall continue to be the querulous victims of the organizations we design to serve us until we gain a deeper understanding of organization. Just as modern ecologists use knowledge of the balance of nature to fight insect pests, using natural forces to fight natural forces, so the student of society may use a knowledge of organization to organize for freedom.

The phrase "organize for freedom" has a paradoxical sound today when to many intellectuals the very idea of organization seems hostile to individual freedom. But in fact we have been organizing for freedom for a very long time. Our legal and constitutional system is, after all, an aspect of social organization designed to protect the individual from mistreatment by others, including the social organization itself.

It is useful to remind ourselves that very few of our freedoms would exist without conscious effort on our part. The majority of us tend to think of freedom as the natural state, and lack of freedom as the unnatural, artificial, contrived state of affairs. We imagine that freedom, like sunshine or fresh air, is always there to be had if someone isn't forcibly preventing us from enjoying it. But freedom as we now know it has been exceedingly rare in the history of mankind. It is a highly perishable product of civilization, wholly dependent on certain habits of mind widely shared, on certain institutional arrangements widely agreed upon. This is worth saying because some moderns are so enamored of the idea of individuality that they would not think of speaking out on behalf of society. They imagine that the only effect a society can have on the individual is a destructive one. But it is by means of the free society that we keep ourselves free. If we wish to remain free, we had better look to the health, the vigor, the viability of our free society—and to its capacity for renewal.

CHAPTER 7

CONDITIONS OF RENEWAL

DEADWOOD AND SEEDBEDS

It is not enough for a society to recognize the need for renewal. It must have the institutional arrangements that make orderly change a possibility.

Many observers have noted that freedom is the existence of alternatives or choices.[1] A society or organization is coercive to the extent that the individual has no alternative to a given path of action. The implications are obvious and underscore the virtues of a pluralistic society—a society in which there are many decision-making points rather than only one, in which power is widely dispersed rather than tightly held. In such a society there is a willingness to entertain diverse views rather than one "official" doctrine. Initiative in political, economic and social matters stems from many sources, rather than only one. Individuals have access to multiple memberships and channels through which they may gain information and express their views.

It would be hard to overemphasize the importance of pluralism in helping a society to escape the cycle of growth and decay. The ever-renewing organization (or society) is not one which is convinced that it enjoys eternal youth. It knows that it is forever growing old and must do something about it. It knows that it is always producing deadwood and must, for that reason, attend to its seedbeds. The seedlings are new ideas, new ways of doing things, new approaches. If all innovations must pass before one central decision point, they have just one chance to survive and a slim one at that. In an organization with many points of initiative and decision, an innovation stands a better chance of survival; it may be rejected by nine out of ten decision makers and accepted by the tenth. If it then proves its worth, the nine may adopt it later.

A free society is not the only kind that can accomplish continuous renewal. Far from it. A totalitarian regime coming to power on the heels of a revolution may be well fitted to accomplish one great burst of change. But in the long run its spurt of energy is in danger not only of dying out but of being replaced by deadly rigidity. Compared to the free society, it is not well fitted for continuous renewal, generation after generation. This is true for reasons we have already touched on—specifically the absence of those institutional arrangements that make for adaptiveness and flexibility. If a society is dominated by one official point of view, the tentative beginnings of a new point of view may be a matter of devastating strain and anxiety. In a society where there are already various points of view, the emergence of another is hardly noticed. In an open society, freedom of communication ensures that the new ideas will be brought into confrontation with the old.

Historically, major changes in a society have usually involved serious disruption of the social fabric. But an open society is well designed to permit the testing and survival of new ideas. Major changes occur without violence. Of particular importance is the concept of a "loyal opposition"—the idea that there is a legitimate role for those who are loyal to the government but in disagreement with its policies. Also important is the whole range of political, legal and social practices by which a free society adjudicates conflict and ensures that opposing views will work themselves out in a framework of order.

One of the most significant safeguards against monolithic integration is our tradition of the dispersal of power and restraints on power. The power of our government is limited, and even within government there are checks and balances, conflicts, rivalries, countervailing power and many points at which initiative may be exercised. The great corporations compete with one another and with a host of lesser corporations; and they are in many respects hedged in by government and by labor. Labor is very far from enjoying monolithic control even over its own affairs; and it must cope with government and business in achieving its ends.

Obviously the great number of groups, organized and unorganized, that have a share in the wielding of political power makes for fluidity in the society. As these groups combine and recombine, jockey among themselves, gain or lose in status, the society as a whole preserves its flexibility.

There is a mistaken conception of efficiency that sees pluralistic approaches as wasteful and confusing. The need for efficiency is not to be laughed off, of course. In a grim world, free societies must prove their capacity to function efficiently. Extremes of pluralism can lead to utter confusion.

But creative organizations or societies are rarely tidy. Some tolerance for inconsistencies, for profusion of purposes and strategies, and for conflict is the price of freedom and vitality.

Quite as important as the tradition of dispersed power is the tradition of tolerance and intellectual freedom. This permits a pluralism of beliefs, a tolerance of differing traditions and a diversity of intellectual positions that have contributed greatly to the vitality of our national life.

Another important feature of our pluralism is the great variety of organizations to which an individual may belong. He may be at the same time an employee of General Motors, a communicant in the Catholic Church, a dues payer in the auto workers union, a registered Democrat, an American Legionnaire and a member of a neighborhood association. And this means that he has many channels of information, many circles in which he may express his views and find out what is going on. He need never fall into a position in which a single organization dominates every phase of his life.

One of the surest sources of protection for the individual in any organization is the sheer existence of other organizations to which he may move. Multiple organizations in a given field with the possibility of free movement among them lessen the coerciveness of all organizations. Coerciveness will rise when the number of organizations drops too low or free movement among them is seriously hindered.

Before leaving this subject we should remind ourselves that pluralism can work only in a society that has adequate forces of cohesion. Without such cohesiveness, pluralism can produce a splintered society. Similarly, conceptions of freedom that are not linked to conceptions of order are extremely disintegrative of the social fabric. There can be order without freedom, but no freedom without some measure of order. Under conditions of social chaos, the individual can never enjoy certain freedoms that are his as a matter of course in a lawful society. Cicero said, "We are in bondage to the law in order that we may be free."[2] Similarly, in the individual the idea of freedom is inseparable from conceptions of moral responsibility and self-discipline. It is not even a matter of choice, as Burke pointed out: "Men of intemperate minds cannot be free; their passions forge their fetters."

PROTECTING DISSENTERS

When one element in a pluralistic system becomes very powerful in relation to the others, the pluralism of the system itself is in danger. Even with the best of intentions, the dominant element is likely to squeeze out the other elements or render them impotent. When we think of the suppression of diversity we call to mind those totalitarian examples in which the suppression is accomplished by a ruthless minority with a monopoly of power. But it is just as common for diversity to be crushed by an amiable majority. The early proponents of women's rights discovered that their chief obstacle was not the hostile minority who attacked them but the relatively benign majority (including large numbers of women) who sanctioned the attacks. Even a very tolerant majority may be impatient of dissenters.

So we have devised a variety of ways to protect the dissenter. Our civil liberties are a part of that system, and so are Robert's Rules of Order, and grievance procedures and the commonly held view that we should hear both sides of an argument. In short, we have a tradition, a set of attitudes and specific social arrangements designed to ensure that points of view at odds with prevailing doctrine will not be rejected out of hand.

But why be so considerate of dissent and criticism? To answer this question is to state one of the strongest tenets of our political philosophy. We do not expect organizations or societies to be above criticism nor do we trust those who run them to be adequately self-critical. We believe that even those aspects of a society that are healthy today may deteriorate tomorrow. We believe that power wielded justly today may be wielded corruptly tomorrow. We know that from the ranks of the critics come cranks and troublemakers, but from the same ranks come the saviors and innovators. And since the spirit that welcomes nonconformity is a fragile thing, we have not depended on that spirit alone. We have devised explicit legal and constitutional arrangements to protect the dissenter.

Some tolerance of dissent has characterized many human societies and organizations down through the ages. But the deliberate and systematic attempt to make life livable for dissenters is a product of the modern world and the open society. How alien this point of view was in some earlier societies is illustrated in Petrarch's remarks to his patron, the Lord of Padua:

> Thou must not be the master but the father of thy subjects, and must love them as thy children; yea, as members of thy body. Weapons, guards, and soldiers thou mayest employ against the enemy—with thy subjects good will is sufficient. By citizens, of course, I mean those who love the existing order; for those who daily desire change are rebels and traitors, and against such a stern justice may take its course.[3]

Contrast that sentiment with the words of David Brewer, speaking of one of our most hallowed institutions:

It is a mistake to suppose that the Supreme Court is either honored or helped by being spoken of as beyond criticism. On the contrary, the life and character of its Justices should be the object of constant watchfulness by all, and its judgments subject to the freest criticism. . . . Many criticisms may be, like their authors, devoid of good taste, but better all sorts of criticism than no criticism at all. The moving waters are full of life and health; only in the still waters is stagnation and death.[4]

The battle to preserve the freedom to disagree will never end. If our freedom were perfect today, it would begin deteriorating almost immediately. It is in the nature of society that it should, and all we can do is to be vigilant.

Of course, a tradition of freedom is effective only in protecting the nonconformist or innovator from his enemies. There is no way to protect him from his friends. And, unfortunately, the first restraining force for one who steps off the paths of custom and majority opinion is not the lethal gunfire of opponents but the clutching hands of intimates and colleagues.

It is sometimes quite difficult to say who is a conformist and who is not. The diagnosis of conformism is complicated by the fact that there exist large groups which exhibit an intense conformism to a nonconformist position. A member of the Communist party in the United States would not be caught dead having an opinion independent of the party, but he thinks of himself as a nonconformist because the party is at odds with the society at large. Another complication is provided by the nonconformist who is simply against everything that people in general are for. As David Riesman has pointed out, this too is a kind of conformism or modishness.[5] It is just as slavish as any other kind.

It is important to take a balanced view of conformity and

nonconformity. Obviously at any given time the society and all of its institutions are held together by those who conform to established ways and customs. Give them due credit. At the same time at various "growing points" in the society, others are testing new solutions to old problems or solving new problems. And the results don't always conform to custom.

There are certain roles in any society that must be protected with particular care from the pressures of conformism. Artists, writers, scholars, critics and innovators of all sorts must be free to weigh ideas regardless of their conventionality, their acceptability or their traditional value. They must be free to roam. Their minds must be free to envisage all kinds of possibilities.

This is not to say that they must necessarily be antagonistic to the society as a whole. There is a romantic notion of artists, writers or innovators which assumes that they must be hostile to the rest of the society. But what they need is freedom in the area of their creative activity, freedom to speculate, to inquire, to imagine the widest range of possible solutions. In the course of such free exploration they may find themselves in either a dissident or an affirmative position with respect to the society. It is their duty to call them as they see them. As Emerson said of the scholar: "Let him not quit his belief that a popgun is a popgun, though the ancient and honorable of the earth affirm that it be a crack of doom." [6]

CHAPTER 8

ORGANIZING FOR RENEWAL

SYSTEMATIC INNOVATION

The same flexibility and adaptiveness that we seek for the society as a whole are essential for the organizations within the society. A society made up of arteriosclerotic organizations cannot renew itself.

In the millions of words that have been written about the art of managing large-scale organizations the patient reader will find much wisdom concerning the forces that make organizations rigidify and decay. Writers on the art of management have in mind many organizational aims other than those which concern us here, but their writings contain many clues to the secret of renewal and innovation.[1]

Perhaps the most distinctive thing about innovation today is that we are beginning to pursue it systematically. The large corporation does not set up a research laboratory to solve a specific problem but to engage in continuous innovation. That is good renewal doctrine. But such laboratories usually limit their innovative efforts to products and processes. What may be most in need of innovation is the corporation itself. Perhaps what every corporation (and every other organization) needs is a Department of Continuous Renewal that would view the whole organization as a system in need of continuing innovation.

The same incomplete approach to innovation may be seen in our universities. Much innovation goes on at any first-rate university—but it is almost never conscious innovation in the structure or practices of the university itself. University people love to innovate away from home.

Experienced managers know that some organizations can be renewed through new leadership and new ideas. Others need a more massive infusion of new blood or far-reaching organizational changes. Still others can only be renewed by taking them apart and putting them together again. And some cannot be renewed at all.

Some management problems are of particular interest to students of renewal. Consider, for example, personnel problems. Nothing is more vital to the renewal of an organization (or society) than the system by which able people are nurtured and moved into positions where they can make their contribution. In an organization this implies effective recruitment and a concern for the growth of the individual that extends from the earliest training stages through the later phases of executive development. For a society it implies the correction of social and economic conditions that blight and smother talent in childhood; a deeply rooted tradition—going far beyond formal schooling—of the full development of individual potentialities; and the existence of social mobility such that talent from any segment of the population may move freely into significant roles in the society.

In an organization, a well-designed system of personnel rotation will yield high dividends not only in the growth of the individual but in organizational fluidity. Free movement of personnel throughout the organization reduces barriers to internal communication, diminishes hostility between divisions and ensures a freer flow of information and ideas. It contributes on the one hand to versatility of the individual and on the other to fluidity of the organization.

In the same way, both society and the individual profit by the free movement of people from one organization to another, and from one segment of society to another. Our own society gives the impression of complete fluidity, but this is partially deceptive. There is relatively little movement, for example, between government, industry and the academic world—despite some spectacular line-crossers. And mobility between organizations is being diminished by pension plans in which benefits are contingent upon the individual remaining with the same organization.

Another topic in management that will be of special interest to the student of renewal is communication. Management specialists have learned much about the kinds of communication channels necessary to keep a large organization functioning well. They have learned, for example, that effective channels of internal communication can prevent the erection of impenetrable walls between parts of the organization, and by so doing may do much to diminish the number of narrow, overspecialized employees. All of this serves the cause of renewal.

In some instances a reduction in communications may be useful. There are circumstances in which creativity and flexibility are greatly inhibited by excessive demands for coordination, administrative review and endorsement from collateral branches of the organization. Experimental ventures may quickly lose all freshness and imaginativeness if subjected to the withering heat of criticism from more conventional parts of the organization.

Considerations of this sort have led many an industrial corporation to provide some measure of insulation between its research division and the rest of the organization. The Air Force achieved the same effect when it set up RAND and similar research facilities as independent organizations, thus freeing the research activity from the context of forces at work in the larger organization.

FILTERED EXPERIENCE

As organizations (and societies) grow larger and more complex, the people at the top (whether managers or analysts) depend less and less on firsthand experience, more and more on heavily "processed" data. Before reaching them, the raw data—what actually goes on "out there"—have been sampled, screened, condensed, compiled, coded, expressed in statistical form, spun into generalizations and crystallized into recommendations.

It is a characteristic of the information processing system that it systematically filters out certain kinds of data so that these never reach the ones who depend on the system. The information that is omitted (or seriously distorted) is information that is not readily expressed in words or numbers, or cannot be rationally condensed into lists, categories, formulas or compact generalizations by procedures now available to us.

No one can run a modern organization who is not extraordinarily gifted in handling the end products of a modern information processing system. So we find at the top of our large organizations (and at the top of government) more and more people who are exceedingly gifted in manipulating verbal and mathematical symbols. And they all understand one another. It is not that they see reality in the same way. It is that through long training they have come to see reality through the same distorting glasses. There is nothing more heart-warming than the intellectual harmony of two analysts whose training has accustomed them to accept as reality the same systematic distortions thereof.

But what does the information processing system filter out? It filters out all sensory impressions not readily expressed in words and numbers. It filters out emotion, feeling, sentiment, mood and almost all of the irrational nuances of human situations. It filters out those intuitive judgments that are just below the level of consciousness.

So the picture of reality that sifts to the top of our great organizations and our society is sometimes a dangerous mismatch with the real world. We suffer the consequences when we run head on into situations that cannot be understood *except* in terms of those elements that have been filtered out. The planners base their plans on the prediction that the people will react in one way, and they react violently in quite another way.

That is why every top executive and every analyst sitting at the center of a communications network should periodically emerge from his world of abstractions and take a long unflinching look at unprocessed reality. Every general should spend some time at the front lines; every research administrator should spend some time in the laboratory doing research of his own; every sales manager should take his sample case out periodically and call on customers; every politician should get out and ring doorbells.

We should not make the mistake of underrating our information processing systems. They are extraordinarily helpful. But they are incomplete.[2]

MASSIVENESS AND IMMOBILITY

There is a problem in organizing for renewal that has never been adequately dealt with in the literature of management, though all experts are aware of it: how to combat the almost inevitable movement of an organization toward elaborateness, rigidity and massiveness and away from simplicity, flexibility and manageable size. Military history illustrates the problem in an illuminating way. Since ancient times, some military forces have relied on speed, mobility, flexibility, imagination and daring and others have relied on sheer power, numbers, solidity and heavy equipment. Prosperous societies have rarely been able to resist the temptation to substitute the latter for the former. And as armed forces grew larger, as their organization grew more complex, as fortifications grew more massive, they became in some respects just that much more vulnerable to an enemy that had mastered speed, mobility and flexibility of striking power. Over the centuries military thinkers have understood this very well (though ministries of war have rarely lived by it) and have sought through technological innovation to have their cake and eat it too—to have both power and speed, both massiveness and flexibility. But, though technology can overcome much, it cannot easily overcome the vast cumbersomeness of organization that characterizes the armed forces of a major power. That is one reason why one encounters in the history of warfare so many instances in which a small, poorly equipped but flexible and daring guerrilla force has played hob with the massive and magnificently equipped forces of a major power. The major military powers have still not learned how to cope with that sort of opposition.

The problem is not confined to the military; it applies to any and all organizations. If an organization has to choose between massive strength and flexibility, it almost invariably chooses massive strength. It feels impelled to equip itself for every conceivable contingency, even at the cost of an elaborateness that limits adaptability. It finds it easy to grow more complex, difficult to grow simpler; easy to grow cumbersome, almost impossible to become disencumbered.

It is not a problem of sheer size. Most experts now recognize that the large organization need not succumb to the unwieldiness and bureaucratic rigidity that we associate with bigness. They believe that if we keep these dangers in mind and design organizations in such a way as to avoid them, we can enjoy the advantages that characterize many (by no means all!) small organizations—simplicity, easy internal communication, flexibility and adaptiveness—and at the same time benefit by the undoubted advantages of bigness— resources in depth, economies of scale, a relatively high degree of internal diversity and the capacity to meet a great range of eventualities.

But there is not only something in organization that tends toward massiveness, elaborateness, solidity and entrenched power, there is something that glorifies forms and formalities, the superficial and external. Consider education. We think we believe in it passionately, and perhaps we do. Yet we accept all kinds of shoddy education that is no more than going through the motions. We pretend that so many courses, so many credits, so many hours in a classroom, so many books read add up to an education. The same is true of research, on which we now spend billions of dollars annually. We seem immensely satisfied with the outer husk of the enterprise—the number of dollars spent, the size of laboratories, the number of people involved, the fine projects outlined, the number of publications. Why do we grasp so desperately at externals? Partly because we are more superficial than we would like to admit. Perhaps partly because we are too lazy or too preoccupied to go to the heart of the problem. But also because it is easier to organize the external aspects of things. The mercurial spirit of great teaching and great scholarship cannot be organized, rationalized, delegated or processed. The formalities and externals can.

NEW ORGANIZATIONAL FORMS

Our most melancholy thoughts about organization almost always concern the classic large-scale industrial or governmental bureaucracy—a thing of divisions, branches, bureaus and departments, through which flow rivers of memoranda. In terms of status, it is a pyramid, and only a few at the top have the faintest idea what the whole organization is about. This is the organization the novels are written about. This is what is pictured in the organization charts. This is the setting in which the legendary office boy rises steadily to the top.

It really does exist. But taken alone it is an extraordinarily inaccurate picture of modern organization. There are at work in the world today forces that play havoc with the ordered arrangements of the industrial or governmental bureaucracy.

Consider, for example, the rise of the professions, one of the striking developments in modern social organization. The conflict between the professions and the bureaucracies is deeply rooted in the nature of professional functioning. The loyalty of the professional man is to his profession, not to the organization that may house him at any given moment. Compare the physical scientist in a local plant with the non-professional executives in the same plant. Often the people the scientists see as their colleagues are not the nonprofessionals in neighboring offices, but fellow scientists wherever they may be throughout the country, even throughout the world. Through their professional ties with widely dispersed contemporaries, they themselves are highly mobile. But even if they stay in one place their loyalty to the local organization is rarely of the same quality as that of the true organization person.

The rise of the professions means that modern large-scale organization has been heavily infiltrated by people who have an entirely different concept of what organization is about and an entirely different image of their own relationship to it. This can have far-reaching consequences in the way the organization is run, as anyone familiar with the administration of universities and hospitals can testify.

Foes of modern large-scale organization will find it pleasant to reflect on this lack of rapport between the professions and the classic bureaucracy. But they must not imagine that the professions are wholly dependable allies. The professions themselves have rather considerable potentialities for rigidifying the society.

Another development that has profoundly altered the nature of the classic bureaucracy is the extraordinary rise of servicing organizations. The large modern organization is invaded every hour of the day and night by armies of people performing one or another sort of service. Just as the crocodile has a bird that picks its teeth and parasites in its digestive tract, so the modern large-scale organization is picked over and used as a supporting environment by an incredible variety of outsiders. Lawyers, auditors, management consultants, architects, decorators, insurance men, bankers, public relations people, advertising people, security people, janitorial services, landscape architects and an endless list of others move in to contribute their highly specialized bits to the complex functioning of the whole—and then move out again. They are a vital part of the human environment and the functioning of the machinery, yet they never appear on the organization chart, and their only relationship to the organization is of a contractual nature.

The remarkable range of such professional and technical services that are available, plus the flexibility of the contractual relationship, gives the modern organization a wide range of choice in shaping its own future. Within limits, top management can put its finger on almost any function within the organization and decree that henceforth that function will be performed by an outside organization on contract. For the organization that wishes to maintain the maneuverability so essential to renewal, this offers priceless opportunities (and some hazards).

Particularly interesting are those instances in which the very nature of the large organization makes it necessary to reach outside for assistance. Much of the effectiveness of the management consultants, for example, is traceable to their "outsideness." Much that they do could—in theory—be done by specialists within the organization, but they have the advantage of operating outside the stultifying forces that afflict insiders. They can take a fresh view. They can speak out. And they *may* be listened to.[3]

Furthermore, since professionals often do not enjoy life

in the large organization and do enjoy the environment of a professional team, the servicing organization is often able to retain a higher grade of specialist than its clients could normally recruit or hold.

Still another development that does not fit the conventional concept of organization is the emergence of associations or federations with strictly limited objectives. A number of doctors band together for the purpose of sharing certain central services—office facilities, laboratory equipment and staff, physical maintenance and the like. A number of independent taxicab owners band together to obtain common garage facilities, accounting services and insurance. A number of small colleges form an association to pool their money-raising efforts.

The possible significance of such arrangements is very great. It is becoming increasingly doubtful that a large number of small, unaffiliated operators can survive in a world of gargantuan organizations. Thus it becomes critically important to explore any possible arrangements by which the individual or small organization can enjoy some of the benefits of large-scale organization without any substantial loss of autonomy.

One could go on at some length enumerating the varied organizational forms that lend a kaleidoscope quality to our national life. The exuberant variety is increased by our national habit of forming voluntary associations to accomplish almost every conceivable shared purpose. Some of these—unions, political parties, professional associations, interest groups—are very powerful indeed. A number of writers have stressed the importance of such associations in the functioning of our kind of free society.[4]

CHAPTER 9

INDIVIDUALITY AND

ITS LIMITS

ESTRANGEMENT FOR ALL

If one had to select a single conception that is central to the consensus in our own society, it would be the idea of the dignity and worth of the individual. The individual is not just so many pounds of assorted chemicals plus a bucket of water. The person is not just a link in a genetic chain or an element in a biological-social system; not just a "resource" (as in the phrase "human resources") that may be used to strengthen the social group. There is not only something important about the individual, there is something inviolable. At the most basic level this involves a right to life and to security of person; but it involves more. There are limits beyond which one's privacy should not be invaded, one's individuality not threatened, one's dignity not impaired.

Yet humans are social beings, and to discuss individuality

without talking about the social system that makes it possible is to talk nonsense. It will be useful for us to examine more closely the relationship of the individual to the group.

Most human beings who have trod the earth have been rather completely embedded in the culture of their community. The testimony of historians on earlier periods and of anthropologists on contemporary primitive societies agrees on this point. Persons embedded in a traditional society hardly think of themselves as separate or separable from their group. They are engulfed by their culture. They accept the traditions, beliefs and ways of life of their group so completely that they are not even aware that they are accepting them. They are culturally defined.

For such people, their community is for all practical purposes "the world." Daniel Lerner found that when Turkish villagers were asked, "If you could not live in Turkey, where would you want to live?" they could not answer the question because they could not imagine living anywhere else. They could more easily imagine destroying the self ("I would rather die") than separating that self from its familiar context.[1]

Although such embeddedness places severe limits on individuality and freedom as we think of them, the men and women involved are not conscious of these limits. It is said that the last thing a fish would be conscious of would be water. Embedded persons swim just as innocently in the culture of their community.

Such embeddedness cannot exist unless the community enjoys some degree of insulation from other cultures. Even in the ancient world there were relatively cosmopolitan centers in which a good many individuals were by no means embedded in their culture. One need only call to mind Plato, who viewed his society with the cool eye of a physician studying a difficult patient.

In the light of these facts it is not strictly accurate to say—as some writers do—that "the emergence of the individual" came with the Renaissance. What does date from the Renaissance is the appearance of persons who made a considerable point about their individuality—who were even, one might say, rather theatrical about it. The people of the Renaissance found that it was exciting not only to be an individual but to talk about it, to preen one's self on it and to build a life around it.

The premonitions of modern individualism in the Renaissance were amply confirmed in the course of the next three centuries. The Reformation, the rise of science, the Enlightenment, the Industrial Revolution—each in its way contributed powerfully to the dissolution of embeddedness as a social norm. Only as this process gained ground did it become possible to think of the free society as we conceive it today—a society in which every person is encouraged and expected to become a free and morally responsible individual.

By the nineteenth century the stage was set for some of the more extreme manifestations of the modern cult of the individual. We encounter on a wide scale the individual who is intensely conscious of—even preoccupied with—his individuality. Kierkegaard said, ". . . if I were to desire an inscription for my tombstone, I should desire none other than 'That individual.' " [2] We encounter individuals who harbor an intense and explicit hostility toward their own society, individuals capable of the deepest feelings of alienation with respect to their community.

The rebellious individualists of the nineteenth century paved the way for an army of followers. The circumstances of modern life are highly favorable to the achievement of certain kinds of individual detachment and autonomy. Mobility is one such circumstance; traditions are apt to be strongly linked to family and locality, and cannot maintain their strength among a transient population. Urbanization and modern communications produce a confrontation of differing traditions. In the resulting confusion of voices, the hold of all traditions is weakened. Under such conditions the authority of the church diminishes, as does the authority of parents. In addition, a powerful literature of rebellion and dissent has accumulated and is available to all young people.

By the time the nineteenth century was finished, any young people intelligent enough and literate enough to know their own tradition could rebel in the grand manner. Today it doesn't even require intelligence or education. The opportunity for estrangement has been fully democratized.

ESCAPE FROM WHAT?

Against this background observers at the beginning of the twentieth century might easily have believed that the path was leading on to ever loftier heights of individual autonomy. But they would have been wrong. Two major developments of the twentieth century forced us to reexamine that view. First, it became apparent that modern mass society was placing new restraints on the individual, a subject we have already discussed. Second, new totalitarian forms emerged and enjoyed considerable success. Most contemporary discussions of the individual and the group are attempts to cope with one or the other of these developments.

It is not easy for young people today to comprehend the shocking impact on free people everywhere of the rise of modern totalitarianism. In the eighteenth, nineteenth and early twentieth centuries, the idea had become more and more widespread that we were indeed progressing toward freedom. It was believed that slowly but surely we were liberating ourselves from benighted traditions, tyrannical social institutions and power-hungry rulers. Then in the face of twentieth-century totalitarianism the ideology of freedom that had grown into such a sturdy plant over the centuries appeared to wither. The depressing thought occurred to many observers that there might be something in human nature that was not, after all, antagonistic to tyranny; perhaps even something that welcomed it.

That this is not strictly a modern phenomenon is emphasized by E. R. Dodds in describing the rising vogue of astrology in Greece in the second century B.C.:

> ... For a century or more the individual had been face to face with his own intellectual freedom, and now he turned tail and bolted from the horrid prospect—better the rigid determinism of the astrological Fate than that terrifying burden of daily responsibility.[3]

In short, it is necessary to examine the capacity of individuals to accept the responsibility of freedom and the conditions under which they will sacrifice their freedoms to gain other objectives. These were the questions, among others, that concerned Erich Fromm in *Escape from Freedom*.[4] In that memorable book, Fromm was particularly interested in discovering why the Nazi and Fascist movements of the 1930's found it so easy to win adherents. He explained it by pointing out that people who submit willingly to an authoritarian regime relieve themselves of the anxieties and responsibilities of individual autonomy. Eric Hoffer, in *The True Believer*, explored the same thesis.[5]

Before we comment further on that view, it might be well to pause for some common-sense reflections on individual autonomy. One frequently encounters the romantic notion that the individual can be master of himself and his fate, divested of all hampering ties, a free-soaring bird. Such notions create grave confusion. Complete individual autonomy is unthinkable. The dictum of Theocritus, "Man will ever stand in need of man," is borne out by all of modern psychology and anthropology. Our social character is fixed in our biological nature. For at least the first half dozen years of life human infants are utterly dependent on their elders. By the time those years have passed they possess deeply rooted social habits. And beyond that, all that makes us most human —communication, self-awareness, sympathy, conscience—is dependent on interaction with other beings of our own kind. So, although we cannot accept the totalitarian notion that our highest fulfillment is to become a faceless member of the group, neither can we accept romantic notions of complete individual autonomy.

For two generations now we have seen (but have not always understood) that when modern civilization loosens the ties that bind the individual to tradition and family, it may result in greater freedom or it may result in alienation and loss of a sense of community. Similarly, when individuals seek autonomy they may achieve freedom and moral responsibility or they may achieve only aggrandizement of the self, with all the accompanying disorders of self-regard: cancerous pride, uncontrolled inflation of self-evaluations, unfulfillable self-expectations.

Most human beings *are* capable of achieving the measure of autonomy and mature individuality required by our conceptions of individual dignity and worth. But certain kinds of separation of *the self* from *all that is beyond the self* are inherently destructive and intolerable to human beings.

It is important to keep these facts in mind when we use the phrase "escape from freedom." Unless we specify what the individual is running away from and what form the running away takes, we may conceal under one label a wide range of distinctive behavior patterns.

It makes a great deal of difference whether the individual is really running away from freedom—i.e., from the moral responsibility of individual choice—or from the meaningless isolation that modern life so often thrusts on us and the arid egocentrism into which we are so often driven by romantic notions of individualism. If it is the latter, then the flight is justifiable, and the only question is what the individual chooses to run *to*. Some will make the catastrophic mistake of submerging their individuality in mindless conformity to a cause or group. Others will be wise enough to relate themselves—as free and morally responsible individuals—to the larger social enterprise and to values that transcend the self. This will be difficult if the larger social enterprise is so fragmented or decayed that they cannot in fact relate themselves to it.

Mature persons must achieve a considerable measure of independence if they are to meet the standards implicit in our ideals of individual freedom and dignity; but at the same time they must acknowledge the limitations of the self, come to terms with their membership in the society at large and give their allegiance to values beyond their own needs.

Some modern intellectuals have not been at all helpful in clarifying these paradoxical facts. Oppressed by the threats to individuality inherent in our modern highly organized society and frightened by the specter of the organization man, they have tended to resent any hint that the individual is not sufficient to himself.

A significant relationship between the self and values that lie beyond the self is not incompatible with individual freedom. On the contrary, it is an essential ingredient of the inner strength that must characterize the free person. People who have established emotional, moral and spiritual ties beyond the self gain the strength needed to endure the rigors of freedom. Let us not doubt that those rigors exist and that the strength is needed. Learned Hand was correct when he said that freedom is a burden to all but the rare individual.[6]

The moral for all of us is clear. We have a duty to nourish those qualities within ourselves that make us free and morally responsible beings. And we have an equally compelling duty to honor values beyond the self.[7]

Paul Tillich, who has explored these relationships more profoundly than any other contemporary thinker, points out that the seemingly contradictory requirements of self-affirmation and commitments beyond the self are most nearly resolved when man sees himself as reflecting a larger harmony, as a bearer of the creative process of the universe, as a microcosmic participant in the creative process of the macrocosm.[8]

THE NATURE OF OUR TASK

Let us now be as clear and as explicit as possible about the dilemmas we face in bringing about an appropriate relationship between the individual and the group.

This is a day of inner estrangement and outer conformity, and we must combat both. On the one hand, the processes of modern society have placed subtle and powerful restraints on the individual. At the same time—and this is the confusing part—other aspects of modern life are slicing through the moorings that relate the individual to his own tradition, to his own group and to the values that lie beyond the self. It is as though a deep-sea diver were to find his movements constricted by more and more ropes binding him to the mother ship, but at the same time to find that his air hose had been cut. All the constricting ties intact, the one life-giving tie severed!

This defines our task. We must combat those aspects of modern society that threaten the individual's integrity as a free and morally responsible being. But at the same time we must help the individual to re-establish a meaningful relationship with a larger context of purposes.

In the process of growing up young people free themselves from utter dependence on others. As the process of maturing continues they must also free themselves from the prison of utter self-preoccupation. To do so we need not surrender our individuality. But we must place it in the voluntary service of larger objectives. If something prevents this outcome, individual autonomy will sour into alienation or egocentrism.

Unfortunately, we have virtually no tradition of helping individuals achieve such commitment. We now have a fairly strong tradition of helping them to detach themselves from the embeddedness of childhood. Most teachers make a conscious effort to help youngsters outgrow the unexamined beliefs of childhood. They jolt them out of hand-me-down attitudes and force them to think for themselves.

Just as we help them in this way to achieve independence, we must later help them to relate themselves to their fellow beings and to the best in their social, moral and intellectual tradition. If we address ourselves to this task, we shall soon discover that one of the reasons young people do not commit themselves to the larger social enterprise is that they are genuinely baffled as to the nature of that enterprise. They do not really understand their own free society. They do not know their own social and intellectual tradition. They do not understand the requirements and realities of a complex modern society. They do not see where they fit in. If they are to commit themselves to the best in their own society, it is not exhortation they need but instruction.

We must also help the individual to discover how such commitments may be made without surrendering individuality. We must help him to understand and resist any impulse he may have to flee the responsibility of individual choice by mindless submission to a Cause or Movement. In short, he must recognize the hazard of having no commitments beyond the self and the hazard of commitments that imperil the self.

If we succeed in our delicate task, then we shall no longer need to agree with Yeats' grim comment on the modern world:

> The best lack all conviction, while the worst
> Are full of passionate intensity.[9]

CHAPTER 10

COMMITMENT AND MEANING

INDIVIDUAL COMMITMENT

In maturity, then, one undertakes commitments to something larger than the service of one's "convulsive little ego," to use William James' memorable phrase—religious commitments, commitments to loved ones, to the social enterprise and to the moral order. In a free society we shall never specify too closely what those commitments should be.

Young people today would have a far easier time understanding the role of commitment in their lives if they were not misled by the juvenile interpretation of the "pursuit of happiness" that is widely held today. It is not unduly harsh to say that the contemporary idea of happiness cannot possibly be taken seriously by anyone whose intellectual or moral development has progressed beyond that of a three-week-old puppy. From Aristotle to Jefferson, philosophers who have thought seriously about happiness would be startled to discover how that word is now interpreted.

The truth is that few humans are capable of achieving

the vegetative state implied in the current conception of happiness. Despite almost universal belief to the contrary, gratification, ease, comfort, diversion and a state of having achieved all one's goals do not constitute happiness for humans. The reason Americans have not trapped the bluebird of happiness, despite the most frantic efforts the world has ever seen, is that happiness as total gratification is not a state to which we can aspire. The irony is that we should have brought such unprecedented dynamism to the search for such a static condition.

It might be possible for an impoverished nation to harbor the delusion that happiness is simply comfort and pleasure and having enough of everything. But we have tried it, and we know better.

One can accept this fact without at the same time under-rating the pleasant things in life. One is rightly suspicious of those who tell poor people that they should be content with poverty, or hungry people that hunger is ennobling. Every human being should have the chance to enjoy the comforts and pleasures of good living. All we are saying here is that they are not enough. If they were, the large number of Americans who have been able to indulge their whims on a scale unprecedented in history would be deliriously happy. They would be telling one another of their unparalleled serenity and bliss instead of trading tranquilizer prescriptions.

So we are coming to a conception of happiness that differs fundamentally from the storybook version. The storybook conception tells of desires fulfilled; the truer version involves striving toward meaningful goals—goals that relate the individual to a larger context of purposes. Storybook happiness involves a bland idleness; the truer conception involves seeking and purposeful effort. Storybook happiness involves every form of pleasant thumb-twiddling; true happiness involves the full use of one's powers and talents. Both conceptions of happiness involve love, but the storybook version puts great emphasis on being loved, the truer version more emphasis on the capacity to give love.

This more mature and meaningful view opens up the possibility that one might even achieve happiness in striving to meet one's moral responsibilities, an outcome that is most unlikely under the present view unless one's moral responsibilities happen to be uncommonly diverting.

Note that we speak of happiness as involving a "striving toward" significant goals, not necessarily the attaining of those goals. It is characteristic of some kinds of human striving that the goals may be unattainable. Those who dedicate their lives to the achieving of good government or to the combating of human misery may enjoy small victories but they can never win the longer battle. The goal recedes before them. Such striving, says Allport, "confers unity upon personality, but it is never the unity of fulfillment, of repose, or of reduced tension." [1]

For this reason, self-renewing people never feel that they have "arrived." They know that the really important tasks are never finished—interrupted, perhaps, but never finished—and all the significant goals recede before one. Those who think that they have "arrived" have simply lost sight of those goals (or perhaps never saw them in the first place).

It is widely believed that humans in their natural state will do only what is required to achieve strictly physical satisfactions; but, as every anthropologist can testify, this is not true. Primitives are intensely committed to their social group and to the moral order as they conceive it. One has to be fairly well steeped in the artificialities of civilization before one can imagine that indulgence of physical satisfactions might be a complete way of life.

Anyone can see that most men and women are quite prepared to (and do) undergo hardship and suffering in behalf of a significant goal. Indeed, they often actually court hardship in behalf of something they believe in. "Virtue will have naught to do with ease," wrote Montaigne. "It seeks a rough and thorny path." [2]

This is not to say that the aims that humans conceive beyond the needs of the self are necessarily ones that would win our admiration. They may be expressions of the highest idealism or they may be crude, even vicious. That is a salient feature of the problem. If we make the mistake of imagining that only the material wants of people need be satisfied and offer them no significant meanings, they are likely to seize upon the first "meanings" that present themselves, however shallow and foolish, committing themselves to false gods, to irrational political movements, to cults and to fads. It is essential that the human hunger for dedication find worthy objects.

It would be wrong to leave the implication that we are selfless creatures who only wish to place ourselves at the service of some higher ideal. Having rejected the oversimplified view of our nature as wholly materialistic and selfish, we must not fall into the opposite error. Humans are complex and contradictory beings, egocentric but inescapably involved with their fellow beings, selfish but capable of superb selflessness. We are preoccupied with our own needs, yet find no meaning in life unless we relate ourselves to something more comprehensive than those needs. It is the tension between our egocentrism and our social and moral leanings that has produced much of the drama in human history.

Of course one always thinks one's neighbor should be more

dedicated. Our own passion for dedication is contaminated by selfishness, laziness and inconstancy, but our ardor for the other fellow's dedication is pure and undefiled. The employer believes that employees should be more dedicated to their work (meaning usually that they should work harder for less pay). Older people think young people should be more dedicated. We are all familiar with the moral zeal that rises in our breast when we think of the standards the other fellow ought to live up to. Artemus Ward said, "I have already given two cousins to the war, and I stand ready to sacrifice my wife's brother. . . ."

Nothing that is said here should be taken as an encouragement of such vicarious morality. Nor is anything that we say here to be taken as a defense of other misguided forms of commitment. There will never be a way of preventing fools from dedicating themselves to silly causes. There is no way to save some intense and unstable minds from a style of dedication that is in fact fanaticism.

Aside from these obvious dangers, there are other more subtle hazards in dedication. Anyone who thinks, for example, that a determination to "do good to others" is not accompanied by certain hazards should remember Thoreau's comment: "If I knew . . . that a man was coming to my house with the conscious design of doing me good, I should run for my life."[3] Doing good to others may be an expression of the purest altruism or it may simply be a means of demonstrating one's superiority or of living vicariously.

HUNGER FOR MEANING

Humans are in their nature seekers of meaning. They cannot help being so any more than they can help breathing or maintaining a certain body temperature. It is the way their central nervous systems work.

In most societies and most ages, however primitive they may have been technologically, the hunger for meaning was amply served. Though some of the religions, mythologies, and tribal superstitions with which the hunger for meaning was fed were crude and impoverished, they did purport to describe a larger framework in terms of which one's life gained significance.

With the arrival of the modern age a good many misguided souls conceived the notion that we could do without such nourishment. And for a breath-taking moment it did seem possible, in view of the glittering promises that modern life offered. Under the banner of a beneficial modernity, the individual was to have security, money, power, sensual gratification and status as high as anyone. He would be a solvent and eupeptic Walter Mitty in a rich and meaningless world.

But even (or especially) those who came close to achieving the dream never got over the nagging hunger for meaning.

At one level, our search for meanings is objectively intellectual. We strive to organize what we know into coherent patterns. Studies of perception have demonstrated that this tendency to organize experience is not an afterthought or the result of conscious impulse but an integral feature of the perceptual process. At the level of ideas, our inclination to organize meaningful wholes out of our experience is equally demonstrable. We try to reduce the stream of experience to orderly sequences and patterns. We produce legends, theories, philosophies.

To an impressive degree, the theories of nature and the universe that we have developed are impersonal in the sense that they take no special account of our own aspirations and status (though they are strictly dependent on our conceptualizing power and rarely wholly divorced from our values). Out of this impersonal search for meaning has come modern science.

But we have never been satisfied to let it go at that. We have throughout history shown a compelling need to arrive at conceptions of the universe *in terms of which we could regard our own lives as meaningful.* We want to know where *we* fit into the scheme of things. We want to understand how the great facts of the objective world relate to *us* and what they imply for our behavior. We want to know what significance may be found in our own existence, the succeeding generations of our kind and the vivid events of our inner life. We seek some kind of meaningful framework in which to understand (or at least to reconcile ourselves to) the indignities of chance and circumstance and the fact of death. A number of philosophers and scientists have told us sternly that we must not expect answers to that sort of question, but we pay little heed. We want, in the words of Kierkegaard, "a truth that is true for me." [4] We seek conceptions of the universe that give dignity, purpose and sense to our own existence.

When we fail in this effort we exhibit what Tillich describes as the anxiety of meaninglessness—"anxiety about the loss of an ultimate concern, of a meaning which gives meaning to all meanings." [5] As Erikson has pointed out, the young person's search for identity is in some respects this sort of search for meaning.[6] It is a search for a framework in terms of which young persons may understand their own aims, their relation to their fellow beings and their relation to larger purposes. In our society every individual is free to conduct this search on his own terms and to find, if he is lucky, the answer that is right for him.

MEANING, PURPOSE AND COMMITMENT

There are those who think of the meaning of life as resembling the answer to a riddle. One searches for years, and then some bright day one finds it, like the prize at the end of a treasure hunt. It is a profoundly misleading notion. The meanings in any life are multiple and varied. Some are grasped very early, some late; some have a heavy emotional component, some are strictly intellectual; some merit the label *religious,* some are better described as *social.* But each kind of meaning implies a relationship between the person and some larger system of ideas or values, a relationship involving obligations as well as rewards. In the individual life, meaning, purpose and commitment are inseparable. When one succeeds in the search for identity one has found the answer not only to the question "Who am I?" but to a lot of other questions too: "What must I live up to? What are my obligations? To what must I commit myself?"

So we are back to the subject of commitment. As we said earlier, a free society will not specify too closely the kinds of meaning different individuals will find or the things about which they should generate conviction. People differ in their goals and convictions and in the whole style of their commitment. We must ask that their goals fall within the moral framework to which we all pay allegiance, but we cannot prescribe the things that will unlock their deepest motivations. Those earnest spirits who believe that one cannot be counted worthy unless one burns with zeal for civic affairs could not be more misguided. And we are wrong when we follow the current fashion of identifying moral strength too exclusively with fighting for a cause. Nothing could be more admirable nor more appealing to a performance-minded people such as ourselves. But such an emphasis hardly does justice to the rich variety of moral excellences that humans have sought and occasionally achieved in the course of history.

A good many of the most valuable people in any society will never burn with zeal for anything except the integrity and health and well-being of their own families—and if they achieve those goals, we need ask little more of them. There are other valuable members of a society who will never generate conviction about anything beyond the productive output of their hands or minds—and a sensible society will be grateful for their contributions. Nor will it be too quick to define some callings as noble and some as ordinary. One may not quite accept Oliver Wendell Holmes' dictum—"Every calling is great when greatly pursued"[7]— but the grain of truth is there.

CHAPTER 11

ATTITUDES TOWARD

THE FUTURE

Onward and Upward?

Individuals cannot achieve renewal if they do not believe in the possibility of it. Nor can a society. At all times in history there have been individuals and societies whose attitudes toward the future have been such as to thwart, or at least greatly impede, the processes of renewal.

There is a readily discernible difference between the society (or individual) that is oriented to the future and the one that is oriented to the past. Some individuals and societies look forward and have the future ever in mind, others are preoccupied with the past and are antiquarian in their interests. The former have a vivid sense of what they are becoming, the latter a vivid sense of what they have been. The former are fascinated by the novelty of each day's experience, the latter have a sense of having seen everything.

No society is likely to renew itself unless its dominant

orientation is to the future. This is not to say that a society can ignore its past. A people without historians would be as crippled as an individual with amnesia. They would not know who they were. In helping a society to achieve self-knowledge, the historian serves the cause of renewal. But in the renewing society the historian consults the past in the service of the present and the future.

The society capable of continuous renewal not only is oriented toward the future but looks ahead with some confidence. This is not to say that blind optimism prevails; it is simply to say that hopelessness does not make for renewal.

Throughout most of our history, the view of the future that has prevailed in this nation has been both confident and hopeful. The attitude is well exemplified in Benjamin Franklin. In the year 1729, he tells us, an elderly man with "a wise look and a very grave manner of speaking" stopped at his door in Philadelphia.

> This gentleman asked me if I was the young man who had lately opened a new printing-house. Being answered in the affirmative, he said he was sorry for me, because it was a very expensive undertaking, and the expense would be lost; for Philadelphia was a sinking place, the people already half-bankrupt.[1]

Franklin did not conceal his distaste for such a gloomy view of the future. Like generations of Americans after him, he had extraordinarily cheerful notions of what lay in store for his city, his nation and himself. As for his crabbed visitor, Franklin remarked,

> This man continued to live in this decaying place . . . refusing for many years to buy a house there, because all was going to destruction; and at last I had the pleasure of seeing him give five times as much for one as he might have bought it for when he first began his croaking.[2]

The society capable of continuous renewal not only feels at home with the future, it accepts, even welcomes, the idea that the future may bring change. In 1831 de Tocqueville asked an American sailor why American ships were built to last for only a short time. The sailor replied that "the art of navigation is everyday making such rapid progress, that the finest vessel would become almost useless if it lasted beyond a few years." The explanation struck de Tocqueville as typically American. "I recognize," he wrote, "the general and systematic idea upon which a great people direct all their concerns."[3]

Much more typical of traditional societies throughout the world (and throughout history) is the attitude of the Mexican villager, described by Frank Tannenbaum, who assumes that the worst is to be expected and who speeds the departing traveler by saying, "May you go with God, and may nothing new happen to you."[4]

In a society capable of renewal, people not only welcome the future and the changes it brings but believe they can have a hand in shaping that future. This belief is so widespread among the modern, industrialized nations that we tend to forget that it is by no means universally held. In fact, the view that humans are helpless to alter their fate is probably the more common view—and has been throughout history. Such fatalism is a grave obstacle to renewal. A European agriculturist, speaking of the Indonesian peasants with whom he had been working, said to me recently, "These people don't lack intelligence; they lack motivation. They don't find modern agricultural techniques so difficult; what they find difficult to absorb is our attitude that man can improve his lot by making an effort."

In any society (or institution) there develops a more or less stable set of attitudes toward what is possible. These attitudes inevitably set ceilings for performance. After Roger Bannister ran the first four-minute mile, other runners promptly duplicated the feat. For generations it had been regarded as an unattainable goal, and this attitude served as a barrier. When Bannister removed the obstacle, others promptly followed.

As a society (or institution) matures there is a subtle but pervasive shift in attitudes toward what is possible. The youthful attitude that "anything is possible" is encountered less frequently, and there are more experts on why "it can't be done." The consequences are predictable: fewer mistakes —and less innovation. Confidence born of ignorance and inexperience is not so contemptible a quality as some imagine.

But of course life cannot be lived in utter disregard of the real limitations that surround performance. And in fact the appraisals which most people make of the limits of the possible are based on *some* solid evidence. The fatalism of the Asian peasant is not really surprising, in view of the evidence before him. People will harbor a hopeful view of what they can achieve only if their societies do, in fact, offer some scope for individual accomplishment. If their societies provide them with the opportunity to grow as individuals and to have an impact on their environment, their attitudes will reflect those realities.

OPTIMISM AND PESSIMISM

It will not have escaped the reader that we have been dealing with attitudes that normally go under the labels— the extremely inexact labels—of "optimism" and "pessimism."[5] For the purposes of this discussion, we have dealt with these attitudes rather narrowly. We must now view them in a broader context.

Throughout most of history thoughtful people have taken a rather grim view of man's life on this earth. The Greeks went so far as to suggest that any considerable happiness, success or achievement in one's life might well foretell disaster. Gilbert Murray wrote: "It is a bad look-out for anyone in Greek poetry when he is called a 'happy man.' " [6] And the good news of the gospel was by no means good news for life on this earth. "Man is born unto trouble, as the sparks fly upward."

Then in the eighteenth century there emerged a strikingly different view of the human condition. People came to believe that our life on this earth need not be grim; on the contrary, it might be perfect if only we used our powers of reason to good effect.

The rationalism, optimism and millennialism of the Enlightenment spread into every area of intellectual life like waves from a thrown rock. It was widely believed that we were treading an onward and upward path that would take us inevitably to the perfect society. A little more good will, rationality, science and material progress were all that were needed to bring us safely to Utopia.

Though it is now easy to laugh at such naïveté, the good consequences were considerable. Much of the best that the Western world has accomplished in education, in human welfare, in science and in the creation of civil institutions compatible with justice and decency was accomplished under the spell of those beliefs.

Coming at a time when our national character was being shaped, the spirit of the Enlightenment marked us more deeply than it marked the older nations of the Western world. Combined with the natural buoyancy of a new nation on a new continent, it produced an exuberance of mood that few foreign visitors failed to note. J. Hector St. John Crève-coeur, a Frenchman who took up farming in New York be-fore the Revolution, said, "A European, when he first arrives, seems limited in his intentions as well as in his views. . . . [He] no sooner breathes our air than he forms schemes, and embarks on designs he never would have thought of in his own country."[7]

In these days of fashionable pessimism, the spirit of the Enlightenment has come in for lacerating criticism and much of the criticism has been justified. There can be no doubt that our traditionally optimistic attitudes prepared us very inadequately for the tragedy, brutality and turbulence of the twentieth century. Minds bred to anticipate the rule of reason were ill equipped to face a world of rampant irration-ality and hatred. Minds attuned to the idea of progress had no way of coping with the retrogressive horrors of Dachau and Buchenwald. Men and women with an extravagant belief in their capacity to govern their fate found it difficult to deal with (or even think about) the vast social forces that were reshaping the world.

FASHIONABLE PESSIMISM

The road back from the optimism of the Enlightenment is familiar to all literate moderns. Men such as Kierkegaard and Dostoevsky foreshadowed the change of mood. Freud, a passionately rational man, struck a devastating blow at the widely prevalent belief in man's rationality. And then the grim events of the twentieth century unrolled—the butchery of World War I, the brutal suppression of freedom in the Communist revolution, the moral obscenities of Nazism and

Fascism, and then World War II, the gas chambers and the bomb.

It is hardly surprising that men and women today take a less cheerful view of the world than their grandparents did. But for some of our contemporaries the pendulum has swung so far toward a bleak and despairing view of life that one may ask whether it has reached the end of its arc. One is inclined to hope so as one contemplates the excessive, self-dramatizing and essentially romantic pessimism that characterizes some modern writers, artists and thinkers. The avant-garde playwright Ionesco sees nothing in the world but "evanescence and brutality, vanity and rage, nothingness or hideous, useless hatred. . . . cries suddenly stifled by silence, shadows engulfed forever in the night."[8] To Cèline, men are "monkeys with a gift of speech"; to Beckett, they are "bloody, ignorant apes" and a "foul brood"; to Rexroth, "life is just a mess, full of tall children, grown stupider."[9] Faced with such self-defilement and dejection, one longs for a little of the old buoyancy, at whatever price.[10]

Our generation is not the first to discover the chance and tragedy of this world, but if some of these writers had their way it might be the first generation to drown in self-pity at the thought. "Of all the infirmities we have," Montaigne said, "the most savage is to despise our being."[11]

Life is harsh, but it has always been harsh. The only sensible view of life is, and has always been, based on a clear-eyed recognition—not necessarily acceptance—of the elements of tragedy, irony and absurdity in life. It is based too on a recognition of one's own limitations and weaknesses, the inexorable facts of the life cycle and all the sorrows, irrationalities and indignities that afflict the flesh and the spirit. Anyone who does not recognize all of that is either very young or very foolish, possibly both. It is not easy to see why so many intellectuals of the twentieth century should agonize and attitudinize about circumstances that hundreds of generations have lived through without comparable self-pity.

One difficulty is that our moral aspirations rise more rapidly than our performance. Given relatively modest advances in the justice and decency of human life, we are soon dreaming that we can fashion a perfectly just and decent world. And that is a conviction that is certain to bring some measure of disillusionment. Charles Frankel has said:

> The revolution of modernity has . . . been a moral revolution of extraordinary scope, a radical alteration in what the human imagination is prepared to envisage and demand. And it has changed the basic dimensions in which we measure happiness and unhappiness, success and failure. It has given us the sense that we make our own history; it has led us to impose new and more exacting demands on ourselves and our leaders; it has set loose the restless vision of a world in which men might be liberated from age-old burdens, and come to set their own standards and govern their own lives.[12]

Held within reasonable bounds such vaulting hopes prevent complacency about past achievements and drive us toward higher goals. But when they get out of hand these volatile aspirations lead us on a wild roller-coaster ride between soaring dreams that life can be perfect and sour-stomached disillusionment when the dreams fail to materialize.

Sensible people will understand that there will never be a time when we are not in imminent danger. Cruelty, violence and brutality will be held in leash only by unresting effort—if held in leash at all. Sloth, indulgence, smugness, torpor begotten of ease and flabbiness begotten of security will always lurk in wait. Rigidity, emptiness of spirit, narrow conventionality and stuffed-shirtism are diseases that may attack any society. No society will ever solve the issue of the individual versus the organization. No society will ever discover how to become civilized without running the risk of becoming overcivilized. No society will ever resolve the tension between equality and excellence.

EXUBERANCE REAPPRAISED

Anyone who understands the requirements of continuous renewal will regard the trend away from optimism as a mixed blessing at best. One must admit that in the past our optimism was often excessive, sometimes to the point of silliness. But before we accept the verdict fashionable in some circles today that it was all a deplorable mistake we had better reflect on the matter.

If we can set aside both the old millennialism and the new dejection and look at the matter from the standpoint of social and individual renewal, there can be no question where the positive values lie. Where growth and creativity are concerned, a certain buoyancy is absolutely essential. One would not wish to return to the uncritical optimism that swept the Western world in the eighteenth and nineteenth centuries— as A. E. Housman put it, "The house of delusions is cheap to build but drafty to live in"[13]—but neither can one welcome the corrosive melancholy so fashionable in some quarters today. A mood of wise and weary disenchantment may seem wonderfully mature, but it does not account for much of the growth and movement and vital action in the world.

Most Americans have never really succumbed to the modern dejection and world-weariness. André Maurois once said of Americans, "In a word, they are optimists," and the judgment still holds good.[14] I do not regard it as an indictment. The capacity of our people to believe stubbornly and irrepressibly that this is a world worth saving, and that intelligence and energy and good will might save it, is one of the most endearing and bracing of American traits.

No sensible person relishes the immature aspects of our optimism but if we lose that optimism we will surely be a less spirited people, a less magnanimous people and an immeasurably less venturesome people. Zest and generosity will disappear from our national style. And our impact on the world may well disappear along with them.

CHAPTER 12

MORAL DECAY AND RENEWAL

THE CONSENSUS IN A FREE SOCIETY

It should now be apparent why anyone concerned for the continuous renewal of a society must be concerned for the renewal of that society's values and beliefs. Societies are renewed—if they are renewed at all—by people who believe in something, care about something, stand for something. What about our own values and beliefs?

We might begin by asking whether we have in this country any consensus with respect to values. Many discouraged Americans say that we do not. There are others who assert that we *should not* have such a consensus. The latter are usually persons deeply committed to the freedom of the individual, deeply loyal to pluralism and diversity as a way of life. They dread even the hint of an official philosophy or morality, and fear that to seek any common ground in our values will ultimately diminish diversity.

The first thing to be said is that in any society which functions effectively some measure of consensus *does* exist. Without it the society would simply fly to pieces. No set of laws could prevent chaos in a society that lacked rough agreement on certain moral assumptions.

No system of social arrangements, no matter how cleverly devised, no matter how democratic in character, is adequate to preserve freedom unless it is undergirded by certain habits and attitudes which are shared by members of the society. The claims of society and the claims of the individual will always be in potential conflict. Individual freedom cannot stand against the powerful pressures that are brought against it unless it is supported by deep-rooted habits of thinking and acting. If young persons have been suckled on the legends of a free people, if they have seen their parents and grandparents act in defense of freedom, if tradition instructs them in how free citizens conduct themselves, the chances of freedom are relatively good. Men and women so instructed will "augur misgovernment at a distance, and snuff the approach of tyranny in every tainted breeze."[1]

But freedom must be supported by more than habits and attitudes. Habits and attitudes can be changed. In the modern world there is a continuous clatter from the breaking of old habits; it is one of the characteristic sounds of our time. The idea of freedom, if it is to have durability, must be rooted in our philosophical and religious views. It is not enough to believe that freedom is a comfortable attribute of one's tradition and way of life. One must also believe that it is a right and necessary attribute. This is another way of saying that allegiance to freedom must grow naturally out of one's moral and ethical values.

Our society has always had a measure of consensus with respect to such values and, whatever the critics may say, we have it still.[2] However fragmented our value system may seem, we do in fact agree on certain truths, share certain aims and acknowledge the validity of certain rules. Measured against the whole panorama of human experience as reported by historians and anthropologists, the dominant values in our society represent a moderately narrow range. What looks like disagreement turns out in the broader perspective to be a haggling over details.

Our agreement in these matters is not in any way incompatible with the ideal of diversity. It is of the very essence of our consensus that it is free and rational. It invites criticism and is subject to varied interpretations. It experiences continuing modification and growth. It is free, unforced and fluid.

Everyone does not have to agree in order for the consensus to be effective. It is only necessary that there be rough agreement among a substantial proportion of those men and women whose intelligence, vigor, awareness and sense of responsibility mark them as shapers of the community purpose.

For anyone interested in innovation the consensus is especially important. If a society enjoys a reasonable measure of consensus, it can indulge in very extensive innovation without losing its coherence and distinctive style. Without the durability supplied by the American consensus, our fondness for innovation and diversity would commit us to chaos and disorder.

In a pluralistic society the consensus must necessarily be at what one might call a middle level of values. Obviously it cannot deal with the surface trivialities of manners and daily customs; neither can it sound the depths. It can deal with fairly fundamental values governing man's behavior and with concepts such as freedom and justice. But those values float over still-deeper reaches of philosophic and religious beliefs. They gain their strength from man's deepest views concerning his own nature. When we reach these depths, however, we are in the presence of matters which concern the individual so profoundly that he must not be asked to compromise them.

To force consensus in the depths of belief would be intolerable. To remain preoccupied with the whitecaps on the surface would be meaningless. So a pluralistic society wisely seeks to establish its consensus in the middle depths.

At that level, in our own case, one finds the ideals of freedom, equality of opportunity, the conception of the worth and dignity of the individual, the idea of justice, the dream of brotherhood. The fact that we are not always faithful to these shared values does not indicate confusion nor a failure of the consensus. *We know the values to which we are being unfaithful.* One might ask, "What difference does it make that we agree on our values if we aren't faithful to them?" The answer is that if one is concerned about therapy, it always makes a difference what the patient is suffering from. This society is suffering not from confusion but from infidelity.

To Point a Moral

In the first half of the twentieth century a large number of people came to believe that the intelligent thing to do was to maintain a "scientific" neutrality or agnosticism with respect to values. Here we must be careful not to blame scientists for views that were often pressed most vigorously by individuals with only a smattering of science.[3] It is true that natural and social scientists have found that a neutrality with respect to certain values is essential to their work. For example, they weren't concerned one way or the other about the theological implications of Darwin's theory. They were interested in whether it offered a better framework for known data than had earlier views.

But the notion that neutrality with respect to all values can be extended to all of life is an absurdity. Those who share the notion have never succeeded in acting in their personal lives as though they were wholly agnostic with respect to values. They continue to be morally indignant when someone cheats them and morally outraged when someone slanders them. But though they do not act like moral agnostics in matters affecting their personal interest, they have often done so in matters affecting the community at large. They seem to believe that they should remain neutral in any public discussion of moral values.

This reluctance of some moderns to deal with moral values is intensified by the concept of moral relativity. Dispassionate investigation reveals that our own moral precepts have shifted with the years, and that other societies have other moral precepts. Thus there has arisen the idea that all moral judgments are relative to the context in which the judgments are made. Social scientists have achieved this perspective at the cost of great struggle, and we need not begrudge them the legitimate benefits thereof. But we are entitled to express concern when increasing numbers of people accept it as justification for a sort of moral *laissez faire*—a notion that if one simply tolerates all sorts of values and permits them to come into conflict with one another, something good will come of it. In this view it is not necessary—or perhaps even seemly—to work for the things one believes in, because somehow the competition among values will work the whole thing out. In fact one doesn't even need to believe in any particular values: one simply maintains the position of an interested observer.

To reduce this position to absurdity, imagine the attitude spread to the entire population. Then no one would believe in anything, and everyone would be an observer watching the competition. But there would be nothing for the observers to observe because no one would have any values.

A more elusive difficulty facing this and the immediately preceding generation has been the negativism with respect to moral seriousness that reached its peak early in this century and still affects many educated men and women. Our generation grew up, and our parents grew up, at a time when the leading lights of the intellectual world—artists, writers, scientists, scholars—were waging a knock-down-and-drag-out fight to free themselves of the stifling conventionality of the nineteenth century. These rebels themselves were often intensely moral, indeed striving for a higher morality than they could find in the conventionalities of the day. They believed that there was a fatal element of hypocrisy in all contemporary expressions of idealism, and they came to suspect all sermons and all the well-worn words that express moral values.

At first, pricking the balloons of conventional morality was a rather adventurous exercise for courageous individuals. But it soon became a game that all could play, and almost all did play, with less and less imagination, more and more empty imitativeness.

There is no question that the rigidities of Victorian convention were an obstacle to the creative urges of the twentieth century. But that battle is over, and those who continue to rush into the fray as though the enemy were still formidable are beginning to seem a bit ridiculous. It is understandable, to be sure. We have never been able to resist an extravagant waste of energy in refighting old battles and combating foes long since vanquished. But the more we indulge ourselves in that direction the less likely we are to gird ourselves for real and present battles. We are no longer inhibited by the rigidities of nineteenth-century morality. Zealous wreckers have torn that house down. The question is not one of further pulverizing the fragments but of asking what we intend to do to protect ourselves from the elements.

This alters radically the direction from which we must seek a moral initiative. Once it was the skeptic, the critic of the *status quo,* who had to make a great effort. Today the skeptic *is* the *status quo.* The one who must make the effort is the one who seeks to create a new moral order. Under these circumstances the individual who, out of sheer habit, applies ridicule to any and all expressions of moral earnestness is as old-fashioned as rumble seats and bathtub gin.

Many moderns would rather walk barefoot over hot coals than utter an outright expression of moral concern. They have to say it obliquely, mix it with skepticism or humor, or smother it with pessimism. But embarrassment about the expression of moral seriousness is a disease of people far gone in affectation and oversophistication. Unaffected people will regard it as normal to consult their deepest values and to exhibit an allegiance to those values. And they will expect those values to influence their behavior, within the limits of human fallibility. They will not think it odd or embarrassing to talk about them.

It is a mistake, of course, to equate moral seriousness with dogmatism, solemnity or conformism. Socrates, who was as earnest as a man could be about matters of moral import was far from dogmatic, rarely solemn, and often disrespectful of the "respectable" ideas of his day.

It would be inaccurate to suggest that a serious and clear-headed concern for moral renewal will bring us out onto some sunny upland beyond the troubles that have plagued man since the beginning. Moral seriousness does not resolve complex problems; it only impels us to face the problems rather than run away. Clearheadedness does not slay dragons; it only spares us the indignity of fighting paper dragons while the real ones are breathing down our necks. But those are not trivial advantages.

The Drying Reservoir

Jacques Barzun tells of the little old lady who complained that "the modern thunderstorm no longer clears the air."[4] It is an attitude of mind that is not confined to little old ladies nor to meteorological subjects. Listen to these melancholy lines:

> To whom can I speak today?
>   The gentle man has perished
>   The violent man has access to everybody.
>
> To whom can I speak today?
>   The iniquity that smites the land
>   It has no end.
>
> To whom can I speak today?
>   There are no righteous men
>   The earth is surrendered to criminals.[5]

The writer's abhorrence of the present and his nostalgia for an older, gentler, more righteous time strikes us as very modern. But the poem was not written by a twentieth-century malcontent. It was written by a man contemplating suicide some four thousand years ago in the time of Egypt's Middle Kingdom.

It is one of our abiding characteristics to think that the old virtues are disappearing, the old values disintegrating, the old, good, stern ways no longer honored. Many people today seem to think that our values, our morality as a people, our devotion to virtue and justice resemble a reservoir that was filled long ago (vaguely, about the time of our grandfathers) and has been seeping away ever since. But our grandfathers thought that the reservoir had been filled by *their* grandfathers and had been seeping away ever since. And their grandfathers thought the same. Why isn't the reservoir empty?

The answer is that the moral order undergoes regeneration as well as decay. Joseph Campbell has written:

> Only birth can conquer death. . . . Within the soul, within the body social, there must be—if we are to experience long survival—a continuous "recurrence of birth" to nullify the unremitting recurrences of death.[6]

Nowhere is this more true than in the realm of values. We are always corrupting the old symbols, drifting away from the old truths. Give us a clean, clear, fresh idea or ideal, and we can promise within one generation to render it positively moldy. We smother our values in ritual and encrust them with social observances that rapidly become meaningless. But while some are losing their faith, others are achieving new spiritual insights; while some are growing slack and hypocritical in the moral dimension of their lives, others are bringing a new meaning and vitality to moral striving.

Everyone does not play an equally important role in the re-creation and reshaping of values. But a far greater proportion of the populace than one might think has some share in the process. Amiel said: "Every life is a profession of faith, and exercises an inevitable and silent propaganda. As far as lies in its power, it tends to transform the universe and humanity into its own image. [Every man's] conduct is an unspoken sermon that is forever preaching to others."[7]

Young people do not assimilate the values of their group by learning the words (truth, justice, etc.) and their definitions. They learn attitudes, habits and ways of judging. They learn these in intensely personal transactions with their immediate family or associates. They learn them in the routines and crises of living, but they also learn them through songs, stories, drama and games. They do not learn ethical principles; they emulate ethical (or unethical) people. They do not analyze or list the attributes they wish to develop; they identify with people who seem to them to have these attributes. That is why young people need models, both in their imaginative life and in their environment, models of what —at their best—they can be.

There is a saying popular among intellectuals today that a society utterly secure in its beliefs never talks about them and that a society which constantly reiterates its beliefs is losing its conviction. Perhaps this was true in stable and relatively homogeneous pre-modern societies. It has not been true for *any* modern society. The modern society necessarily talks about its beliefs, argues about them, celebrates them, dramatizes them.

Helping each generation to rediscover the meaning of liberty, justice—"the words on the monuments"—is a perennial task for any society. Each generation is presented with victories that it did not win for itself. A generation that has fought for freedom may pass that freedom on to the next generation. But it cannot pass on the intense personal knowledge of what it takes in courage and endurance to win freedom.

In some cases, young people find that the moral precepts their parents have to offer are no longer relevant in a rapidly changing world. And they often find that in moral matters the precepts their parents utter are contradicted by the behavior their parents exhibit. This is confusing, but not catastrophic. Those writers who imagine that it destroys all possibility of youthful moral striving are wrong. The first task of renewal in the moral sphere is *always* the difficult confrontation of ideal and reality, precept and practice; and young people are very well fitted to accomplish that confrontation. Their freshness of vision and rebelliousness of mood make them highly effective in stripping the encrustations of hypocrisy from cherished ideals.

One of the most difficult problems we face is to make it possible for young people to participate in the great tasks of their time. In a complex technological society such as ours it has become increasingly difficult to find constructive outlets for the imagination and the energies of youth. Alexander might conquer half the known world in his early twenties, and nineteenth-century New England lads might be sailing captains in their late teens, but our age lays enormous stress on long training and experience. We have designed our society in such a way that most possibilities open to the adolescent today are either bookish or frivolous. And all too often when we do seek to evoke his moral strivings the best we can do is to invite him to stand sentinel over a drying reservoir! What an incredibly dull task for the restless minds and willing hearts of young people! It is hardly surprising that many young people think of the moral order as something invented by parents, deans and commencement speakers for the sole purpose of boring the young.

The notion of the drying reservoir is particularly inappropriate because it suggests that the problem is to preserve something that can never be added to. In this way it induces defensiveness and ignores all possibility of creativity. People thinking in terms of the almost empty reservoir will be much too preoccupied with preservation to build creatively for an unknown future.

Instead of giving young people the impression that their task is to stand a dreary watch over the ancient values, we should be telling them the grim but bracing truth that it is their task to re-create those values continuously in their own behavior, facing the dilemmas and catastrophes of their own time. Instead of implying that the ideals we cherish are safely embalmed in the memory of old battles and ancestral deeds we should be telling them that each generation refights the crucial battles and either brings new vitality to the ideals or allows them to decay.

In short, the nurturing of values that maintain society's moral tone—or allow that moral tone to slacken—is going on every day, for good or ill. It is not the dull exercise in ancestral piety that some adults make it seem. It goes on in the dust and clamor of the market place, the daily press, the classroom and the playground, the urban apartment and the suburban ranch house, and it communicates itself more vividly through what men do than through what they say. The moral order is not something static, it is not something enshrined in historic documents, or stowed away like the family silver, or lodged in the minds of pious and somewhat elderly moralists.

It is an attribute of a functioning social system. As such it is a living, changing thing, liable to decay and disintegraton as well as to revitalizing and reinforcement, and never any better than the generation that holds it in trust.

Men and women who understand this truth and accept its implications will be well fitted to renew the moral order— and to renew their society as well. They will understand that the tasks of renewal are endless. They will understand that their society is not like a machine that is created at some point in time and then maintained with a minimum of effort; a society is being continuously re-created, for good or ill, by its members. This will strike some as a burdensome responsibility, but it will summon others to greatness.

NOTES

INTRODUCTION

* John W. Gardner, *Excellence: Can We Be Equal and Excellent Too?* (Harper & Brothers, 1961).

1. GROWTH, DECAY AND RENEWAL

1. Spengler and Toynbee have been severely battered by scholarly critics, but their theories, however vulnerable, are the work of men of great imagination and originality. Anyone seriously interested in the rise and fall of civilizations will read them with profit. (Oswald Spengler, *Decline of the West* [Alfred A. Knopf, Inc.], Vols. I-II, 1945; Arnold J. Toynbee, *A Study of History* [Oxford University Press], Vols. I-XII, 1935-1961.)

2. Arnold Toynbee, "The Graeco-Roman Civilization," *Civilization on Trial* and *The World and the West* (Meridian Books, World Publishing Co., 1958), p. 50.

3. Peter Drucker, *Landmarks of Tomorrow* (Harper & Brothers, 1959), Chaps. 1 and 2.

2. SELF-RENEWAL

1. Of course, the narrowing process is not wholly avoidable. If the process of maturing were not selective and narrowing, one would have no coherence and no focus in one's life. Furthermore, everyone has settled habits that have no great justification except that they are comfortable. The scientist who will discard a pet theory on a moment's notice may fly into a rage if the housekeeper discards his pet pipe. And who knows whether the pet pipe (plus all the other comfortable continuities of his life) provides precisely that margin of security which permits him to lead the reckless life of innovation?

In short, even the self-renewing person has fixed habits and attitudes, but they are not of the sort that interfere with continuous renewal. If the scientist changed his pipe weekly but never his theories, he would be in serious difficulty. The moral is clear. If we must have some continuity in our lives—and we must—let it be of the sort that does not prevent renewal.

2. See D. W. Fiske and S. R. Maddi, *Functions of Varied Experience* (Dorsey Press, Inc., 1961), for some highly relevant data from experimental studies of behavior.

It is customary to belittle the traveler who presumes to give his immediate, unripe impressions of a place he is visiting for the first time. Yet his first impressions may have a freshness and clarity that he will never recapture.

Despite the capacity of travel to bring fresh perceptions, it would be a mistake to suppose that everyone who has stayed in the same place or continued the same style of life has necessarily gone to seed. Thoreau lived as constricted a life as one could imagine and yet found within himself and his immediate environment sources of renewal that have nourished succeeding generations. There is in anyone's normal environment enough depth and variety of human experience, enough complexity of human interaction to place endlessly new demands on the mind and spirit—provided that one has within oneself the gift for constantly searching one's small universe, as did Thoreau, with an undimmed eye and an unhackneyed mind. Unfortunately those are precisely the qualities that most of us fail to preserve as the years pass.

3. For a full discussion of the insatiable demand for talent in a complex modern society, see *Excellence: Can We Be Equal and Excellent Too?*

4. One reason the individual can rarely think clearly about the renewal of society or of an institution to which he belongs is that it never occurs to him that he may be part of the problem, that he may be part of what needs renewing.

5. Anyone interested in this topic would do well to read Abraham Maslow's description of self-actualizing men and women (*Motivation and Personality*). Also relevant is David McClelland's *The Achieving Society*. Neither Maslow nor McClelland is dealing with self-renewing individuals as I have used the term, but much that they have to say is pertinent.

6. Erik H. Erikson, "The Problem of Ego Identity," *Journal of the American Psychoanalytical Association*, Vol. 4, No. 1 (January), 1956.

7. George Herbert, "The Church-Porch," F. E. Hutchinson (ed.), *The Works of George Herbert* (Clarendon Press, 1953), p. 12.

8. Reinhold Niebuhr, "Modern Education and Human Values," Edward Weeks (ed.), from the Pitcairn Crabbe Foundation Lecture Series (University of Pittsburgh Press, 1948), Vol. II, p. 35.

9. Quoted in W. I. B. Beveridge, *The Art of Scientific Investigation* (W. W. Norton, Inc., 1957), Rev. Ed., p. 60.

10. Ralph Waldo Emerson, "The Preacher" (1867), *The Complete Works of Ralph Waldo Emerson* (Houghton Mifflin Co., 1911), Vol. X, p. 229. Two hundred and fifty years earlier Bishop John Jewel said something remarkably similar: "In old time we had treen [i.e., wooden] chalices and golden priests, but now we have treen priests and golden chalices" (*Certain Sermons Preached before the Queen's Majesty* [1609], p. 176). In May, 1849, Emerson wrote in his journal, "I hate quotations."

11. Nothing is more readily observable in the life of organizations than the triumph of form over spirit. Great ventures start with a vision and end with a power structure. One can see in every field—education, religion, business, government, science—the course of events described by Kermit Eby in the labor movement: "The union movement is no longer a fellowship of dreamers sharing one faith and aspiring to a common destiny. Today, big unionism is big business, and its power structure resembles that of the corporation. . . . Efficiency has conquered enthusiasm, statistics have won out over men" (Kermit Eby, *Protests of an Ex-Organization Man* [Beacon Press, 1961], p. 44).

12. The literature on motivation is voluminous, and quite uneven in quality. Beginners can lose a great deal of time in trying to find their way through a maze of scholarly and far-from-scholarly material. One authoritative and discriminating guide to the subject is C. S. Hall and Gardner Lindzey, *Theories of Personality*, Third Edition (Wiley and Sons, 1975).

13. Writing of Rome in its last days of greatness, Rostovtseff said: "That Rome, her civilization, and her political system, were alike immortal—such was the general opinion. There was no one to struggle with and nothing to struggle for. . . . What was there to seek for, when all was already found?" (M. I. Rostovtseff, *A History of the Ancient World* [Clarendon Press, 1928], Vol. 2, p. 364.)

14. David C. McClelland, *The Achieving Society* (Nostrand Co., Inc., 1961).

3. VERSATILITY

1. See Jerome Bruner, *The Process of Education* (Harvard University Press, 1960), for one of the best discussions of an approach to education that might be adequate to the goals of renewal.

2. C. P. Haskins, *Of Societies and Men* (W. W. Norton, Inc., 1951), pp. 95-97.

4. INNOVATION

1. Lyman Bryson, "On Deceiving the Public for the Public Good," in R. M. MacIver (ed.), *Conflict of Loyalties* (Institute for Religious and Social Studies, 1952), p. 12.

2. Lyman Bryson, *The Next America* (Harper & Brothers, 1952), p. 9.

3. Pasteur Vallery-Radot, *Louis Pasteur: A Great Life in Brief* (Alfred A. Knopf, 1958), pp. 84-85.

4. The discussion of creativity in this chapter draws heavily on the research of Frank Barron, Richard Crutchfield, Jacob Getzels, J. P. Guilford, Donald MacKinnon, Morris Stein and others. Creativity is an extraordinarily difficult and elusive research topic, and we owe a debt of gratitude to research workers who have had the courage and ingenuity to tackle it. See Frank Barron, *Creativity and Psychological Health* (Van Nostrand, 1963); Richard S. Crutchfield, "Independent Thought in a Conformist World," in Seymour Farber and Roger H. L. Wilson (eds.) *Conflict and Creativity* (McGraw-Hill, 1963); J. W. Getzels and P. W. Jackson, "The Highly Intelligent and the Highly Creative Adolescent: A Summary of Some Research Findings," in Calvin W. Taylor and Frank Barron, *Scientific Creativity: Its Recognition and Development* (Wiley, 1963); J. P. Guilford, *Personality* (McGraw-Hill, 1959); Donald W. MacKinnon, "The Nature and Nurture of Creative Talent," *American Psychologist*, Vol. 17, No. 7 (July), 1962.

5. "Mozart's growth as a creator was like that of a rare and precious plant, whose innermost secret remains a mystery, but which is nourished by sun and rain and hindered by unfavorable weather." Alfred Einstein, *Mozart: His Character and His Work* (Oxford University Press, 1945).

6. It is not surprising that there is overlap between the traits of the creative and of the self-renewing man. The psychological processes underlying creativity and self-renewal may prove to be very similar.

7. Donald W. MacKinnon in an unpublished memorandum, November, 1955, p. 14.

8. J. P. Guilford, "Creativity," *American Psychologist*, Vol. 5 (1950), pp. 444-454.

9. Anne Roe, *The Making of a Scientist* (Dodd, Mead & Co., 1953).

5. OBSTACLES TO RENEWAL

1. In his autobiography, Thomas M. Storke, Pulitzer Prize-winning publisher of the Santa Barbara *News-Press*, wrote: "In the spring of 1925 the city council adopted a new building code and stricter zoning laws. . . . Hundreds of eyesore buildings still spoiled the aspect of State Street; the city planners estimated that it would take fifty years to remodel or replace them. . . .

"But the benevolent angel who seemed to be watching over our city's destiny decided to wipe out the ugly features in one brief, devastating sweep. She made her visitation in the form of a major earthquake." (Thomas M. Storke, *California Editor* [Westernlore Press, 1958], p. 269.)

2. This is another way of saying that innovation and renewal may be very painful. It is worth reminding ourselves of that fact, because everyone wants renewal but no one wants the pain that goes with it. We make a grave mistake when we give the developing nations the idea that social change is really very easy once one's mind is made up. Though some of the developing nations are "new nations" politically speaking, most of them are in reality old and rather static societies. Renewal will be difficult and it will be painful.

3. In all of these matters of organizational decay, one cannot do better than to study Parkinson. (C. Northcote Parkinson, *Parkinson's Law* [Houghton Mifflin Co.], 1957.)

4. W. I. B. Beveridge, *The Art of Scientific Investigation* (W. W. Norton, Inc., 1957), p. 2.

5. Frederick Jackson Turner, "The Significance of the Frontier in American History" (1893), E. E. Edwards (ed.), *The Early Writings of Frederick Jackson Turner* (University of Wisconsin Press, 1938).

6. Referring to the Lost Generation, Malcolm Cowley wrote:

"Literature, our profession, was living in the shadow of its own great past. The symbols that moved us, the great themes of love and death and parting, had been used and exhausted. Where could we find new themes when everything, so it seemed, had been said already? Having devoured the world, literature was dying for lack of nourishment. Nothing was left to ourselves—nothing except to deal with marginal experiences and abnormal cases, or else to say the old things over again with a clever and apologetic twist of our own. Nothing remained except the minor note." (Malcolm Cowley, *Exile's Return* [Peter Smith, 1959], pp. 18-19.)

7. John Bunyan, *The Pilgrim's Progress* (Winston Co., 1933), p. 169.

8. Malraux said that "the artist is born a prisoner of his style" but he was making quite a different point, viz., that there is no art without style. (A. Malraux, *The Voices of Silence* [Doubleday & Co., Inc., 1953], p. 316.)

9. "I remember, the Players have often mentioned it as an honour to Shakespeare, that in his writing (whatsoever he penn'd) hee never blotted out a line. My answer hath beene, would he had blotted a thousand. . . . Hee was (indeed) honest, and of an open, and free nature: had an excellent Phantsie; brave notions, and gentle expressions: wherein hee flow'd with that facility, that sometime it was necessary he should be stop'd. . . . His wit was in his own power; would the rule of it had beene so too." Ben Jonson, quoted in E. K.

Chambers, *William Shakespeare. A Study of Fact and Problems* (Clarendon Press, 1930), Vol. 2, p. 210.

10. Spengler's writing is laden with nostalgia for a simpler, more vigorous, less complicated world. Rousseau's noble savage is a nostalgic invention. When Nietzsche calls for men to revitalize an aging civilization, he envisages men reminiscent of an earlier stage of civilization— primitive and barbaric in the sense that they are not trapped in the niceties and intricacies of a highly cultivated civilization.

11. Nathaniel Hawthorne, *Notebooks* (March, 1856). At almost the same moment in history, the French Impressionist, Pissarro, was expressing the view that the Louvre ought to be burned. See John Rewald, *The History of Impressionism,* (Museum of Modern Art, 1961).

12. William James, *The Varieties of Religious Experience* Modern Library, (Random House, 1902), p. 313.

6. TYRANNY WITHOUT A TYRANT

1. John Stuart Mill, *On Liberty* (Bobbs-Merrill Co., Inc., 1956).

2. Søren Kierkegaard, *"That Individual": Two "Notes" Concerning My Work as an Author,* 1859. (In Søren Kierkegaard, *The Point of View,* Walter Lowrie (trans.) [Oxford University Press, 1939], p. 115.)

3. Malcolm Cowley, *Exile's Return* (Peter Smith, 1959), pp. 18-19.

7. CONDITIONS OF RENEWAL

1. Charles Frankel, in his very useful book, *The Democratic Prospect* (Harper & Row, 1962), sheds light on this subject and on almost every other significant question in the working of democracy as we know it. See also *The Power of the Democratic Idea* (Doubleday, 1960), a report prepared for the Rockefeller Brothers Special Studies Project by a group under the chairmanship of James A. Perkins, with Charles Frankel doing the drafting.

2. Marcus Tullius Cicero, "Pro Cluentio," *The Speeches of Cicero,* trans. by H. Grose Hodge (Loeb Classical Library, Harvard University Press, 1927), p. 379.

3. Quoted in Jacob Burkhardt, *The Civilization of the Renaissance in Italy* (Modern Library, 1954), p. 8.

4. David Josiah Brewer, Lincoln's Day Address, 1898.

5. David Riesman, *Individualism Reconsidered* (Free Press, 1954), pp. 117-118.

6. Ralph W. Emerson, "The American Scholar," An Oration Delivered before the Phi Beta Kappa Society at Cambridge, 1837.

8. ORGANIZING FOR RENEWAL

1. Interesting accounts of the rise and fall of organizations may be found in the best business periodicals. Peter Drucker's *Managing in Turbulent Times* (Harper and Row, 1980) is a widely read book on the subject.

2. Alfred North Whitehead pointed out that any intellectual system tends to accomplish the sort of filtering of reality that we have described for information processing systems, and is subject to the same dangers. "We all know those clear-cut trenchant intellects, immovably encased in a hard shell of abstractions. They hold you to their abstractions by the sheer grip of personality.

"The disadvantage of exclusive attention to a group of abstractions, however well founded, is that, by the nature of the case, you have abstracted from the nature of things. Insofar as the excluded things are important in your experience, your modes of thought are not fitted to deal with them. You cannot think without abstractions; accordingly, it is of the utmost importance to be vigilant in critically revising your *modes* of abstraction. . . . A civilization which cannot burst through its current abstractions is doomed to sterility after a very limited period of progress." Alfred North Whitehead, *Science and the Modern World* (1925) (New American Library, 1962), p. 58.

3. Kenneth Boulding sees the emergence of the management consultant as an expression of a more general need on the part of top executives to obtain "independent" services and judgments. "This is one reason why organizations develop staff divisions which stand apart from the line hierarchy. It is an important reason for the development of independent suppliers of information: auditors to check on the accountants, management consultants to check on the junior executives, 'Willmark' operatives to check on sales clerks. . . . It is an important reason also for the acceptance of 'tenure' and 'seniority'—devices which . . . [create] a certain necessary independence of the executive." (Kenneth Boulding, "The Jungle of Hugeness," *Saturday Review*, March 1, 1958.) See also Kenneth Boulding, *The Organizational Revolution* (Harper & Brothers, 1953), for a significant examination of some of these problems.

4. For example, Charles Frankel, *The Democratic Prospect* (Harper & Row, 1962).

9. INDIVIDUALITY AND ITS LIMITS

1. Daniel Lerner, *The Passing of Traditional Society* (Free Press, 1958), p. 148.

2. S. Kierkegaard, *op. cit.*, p. 131.

3. E. R. Dodds, *The Greeks and the Irrational* (Beacon Press, 1957), p. 246.

4. Erich Fromm, *Escape from Freedom* (Rinehart and Co., 1941).

5. Eric Hoffer, *The True Believer* (Harper & Brothers, 1951).

6. Learned Hand, *The Spirit of Liberty* (Alfred A. Knopf, 1952). Camus put it more colorfully: ". . . Freedom is not a reward or a decoration that is celebrated with champagne. Nor yet a gift, a box of dainties designed to make you lick your chops. Oh no! It's a chore . . . and a long-distance race, quite solitary and very exhausting. No champagne, no friends raising their glasses as they look at you affectionately. Alone in a forbidding room, alone in the prisoner's box before the judges, and alone to decide in face of oneself or in the face of others' judgment. At the end of all freedom is a court sentence; that's why freedom is too heavy to bear, especially when you're down with a fever, or are distressed, or love nobody." (A. Camus, *The Fall* [Alfred A. Knopf, 1960], pp. 132-133.)

7. Henry A. Murray, "Individuality: The Meaning and Content of Individuality in Contemporary America," *Daedalus*, Vol. 87, No. 3 (1958), pp. 43-44. "Individuality is something to be built for the sake of something else. It is a structure of potential energies for expenditure in the service of an idea, a cultural endeavor, the betterment of man, an emergent value. . . . An individual self is made only to be lost—that is, only to pledge itself to some enterprise that is in league with a good future; and thereby find itself once more."

8. Paul Tillich, *The Courage to Be* (Yale University Press, 1952).

9. W. B. Yeats, "The Second Coming" (1921).

10. COMMITMENT AND MEANING

1. Gordon W. Allport, *Becoming* (Yale University Press, 1955), pp. 66-68.

2. M. E. Montaigne, *Essais*, Maurice Rat (ed.) (Classiques Garnier), Vol. II, p. 100.

3. Henry David Thoreau, *Walden and Civil Disobedience*, Norman H. Pearson (ed.) (Holt, Rinehart & Winston, 1948), p. 55.

4. Søren Kierkegaard, *Journal* (Aug. 1, 1835). In Robert Bretall (ed.), *A Kierkegaard Anthology* (Princeton University Press, 1946), pp. 4-5.

5. Paul Tillich, *op. cit.*, p. 47.

6. "First a word about the term identity. As far as I know Freud used it only once in a more than incidental way, and then with a psychosocial connotation. It was when he tried to formulate his link to Judaism, that he spoke of an "inner identity" which was not based on race or religion, but on a common readiness to live in opposition, and on a common freedom from prejudices which narrow the use of the intellect. Here, the term identity points to an individual's link with the unique values, fostered by a unique history, of his people. Yet, it also

relates to the cornerstone of this individual's unique development: for the importance of the theme of "incorruptible observation at the price of professional isolation" played a central role in Freud's life. It is this identity of something in the individual's core with an essential aspect of a group's inner coherence which is under consideration here: for the young individual must learn to be most himself where he means most to others—those others, to be sure, who have come to mean most to him. The term identity expresses such a mutual relation in that it connotes both a persistent sameness within oneself (self-sameness) and a persistent sharing of some kind of essential character with others." (Erik H. Erikson, *op. cit.*, p. 56.)

7. Oliver Wendell Holmes, "The Law," speech given at the Suffolk Bar Association Dinner, Feb. 5, 1885, *Speeches* (Little, Brown & Co., 1913), p. 17.

11. ATTITUDES TOWARD THE FUTURE

1. Benjamin Franklin, *Autobiography* (Macmillan Company, 1930), p. 91.

2. *Ibid.*, p. 91.

3. Alexis de Tocqueville, *Democracy in America* (1840) (Alfred A. Knopf, 1951), Vol. II, p. 34.

Nothing affects attitudes toward the future more powerfully than what might be termed self-images of growth. The society, organization or individual that sees itself as young and growing will look eagerly to the future. In our early days as a nation, self-images of growth were particularly vivid and affected our whole national temper. In the development of the West one can readily trace the effect of such self-images in generating optimism and receptivity to change.

4. Frank Tannenbaum, *Mexico* (Alfred A. Knopf, 1950), p. 19.

5. For an important research contribution to our understanding of some of the attitudes discussed in this chapter see Florence Kluckhohn and Fred L. Strodtbeck, *Variations in Value Orientations* (Row, Peterson and Co., 1961).

6. Quoted in E. R. Dodds, *op. cit.*, p. 52.

7. J. Hector St. John Crèvecoeur, *Letters from an American Farmer* (1782). (Quoted in Oscar Handlin, *This Was America* [Harvard University Press, 1949], p. 43.)

8. Eugene Ionesco, "Lorsque j'ecris . . . ," quoted in Martin Esslin, *The Theatre of the Absurd* (Doubleday Anchor Books, 1961).

9. L. F. Céline, *Journey to the End of Night* (New Directions, 1960), p. 4; S. Beckett, *Waiting for Godot* (Grove Press, 1954), pp. 9, 51; K. Rexroth, *Bird in the Bush* (New Directions, 1957), p. 157.

10. Of course, in any time of rapid social change a part of the populace will be rightfully gloomy because they are more in tune with

the aspects of their world that are dying than with those that are being born. In a sense, they are a part of what must be renewed, and they may be forgiven for resenting it.

11. M. E. Montaigne, *Essais,* Maurice Rat (ed.) (Classiques Garnier), Vol. III, p. 367.

12. Charles Frankel, *The Case for Modern Man* (Harper & Brothers, 1956), pp. 208-209.

13. A. E. Housman, *Introductory Lecture,* delivered before the Faculties of Arts and Laws and of Science in University College, London, Oct. 3, 1892 (Cambridge University Press, 1937), p. 37.

14. Oscar Handlin, *op. cit.,* p. 567.

It would be wrong, however, to leave the impression that the American mood has always been one of unrelieved cheerfulness. One need only think of Hawthorne, Melville and Henry James to recall another side of the American character.

12. MORAL DECAY AND RENEWAL

1.Edmund Burke, "Speech on Conciliation with America," March 22, 1775.

2. This whole subject is discussed more fully in the author's book *Excellence.*

3. Those who are puzzled about the true relationship of science to the realm of values would do well to read J. Bronowski's brilliant essay on *Science and Human Values* (Harper & Brothers), 1959.

4. Jacques Barzun, *God's Country and Mine* (Vintage Books, 1959).

5. H. Frankfort, *Ancient Egyptian Religion* (Columbia University Press, 1948), p. 73.

6. Joseph Campbell, *The Hero with a Thousand Faces,* Bollingen Series XVII (Pantheon Books, 1949), p. 16.

7. Henri F. Amiel, *Amiel's Journal* (1852), Mrs. Humphry Ward (trans.) (Macmillan & Co., 1889), p. 24.

About the Author

John W. Gardner served as Secretary of Health, Education and Welfare from 1965 to 1968. He then became chairman of the National Urban Coalition and, in 1970, he founded Common Cause. Mr. Gardner resigned as chairman of Common Cause in 1977. From 1978 to 1980 he worked with others to found a new organization, Independent Sector, designed to preserve and strengthen the voluntary sector in American society. He has served as consultant to a number of organizations, among them the Aspen Institute for Humanistic Studies and the United Way of America.

Mr. Gardner was born in Los Angeles in 1912. He attended Stanford University, where he received his A.B. "with great distinction," and his M.A. in psychology. During his undergraduate years, he set a number of Pacific Coast intercollegiate records in swimming; he holds the Distinguished Achievement Medal of the Stanford Athletic Board. He received his Ph.D. from the University of California in 1938 and taught psychology at the University of California, Connecticut College for Women, and Mount Holyoke College.

In 1942 Mr. Gardner served with the Federal Communications Commission. In 1943 he joined the U.S. Marine Corps and was assigned to serve with the OSS in Washington, Italy, and Austria. Mr. Gardner joined the Carnegie Corporation in 1946 as executive associate. In 1955 he became president of the corporation and also of the Carnegie Foundation for the Advancement of Teaching.

Mr. Gardner served continuously from 1947 to 1965 as a consultant to various government agencies: AID, State Department, the U.S. Air Force, the White House, the U.S. Delegation to the United Nations, and others.

He served on President Kennedy's Task Force on Education and was chairman of Kennedy's Commission on International Educational and Cultural Affairs. He was chairman of President Johnson's Task Force on Education and of the White House Conference on Education (1965).

Mr. Gardner was the editor of President Kennedy's book *To Turn the Tide* and is the author of the books *Excellence*, *Self-Renewal*, *No Easy Victories*, *The Recovery of Confidence*, *In Common Cause*, and *Morale*. He is the co-editor, with Francesca Gardner Reese, of *Quotations of Wit and Wisdom (Know or Listen to Those Who Know)*.

Among the boards and councils on which Mr. Gardner has served are the Metropolitan Museum of Art, the Scientific Advisory Board of the Air Force, Shell Oil Company, New York Telephone Company, American Airlines, Time, Inc., and the American Association for the Advancement of Science.

In 1964 Mr. Gardner was awarded the Presidential Medal of Freedom, the highest civil honor in the United States. Among the other awards he has received are the AFL-CIO Murray-Green Award, the United Auto Workers Social Justice Award, the U.S. Air Force Exceptional Services Award, the Public Welfare Medal of the National Academy of Sciences, the Thomas Hart Benton Award of the Kansas City Art Institute, the Democratic Legacy Award of the Anti-Defamation League, The American Board of Professional Psychology Award for Distinguished and Exceptional Service, and honorary degrees from various colleges and universities.